# LISTENING TO PATIENTS

# LISTENING TO PATIENTS

Relearning the Art of Healing in Psychotherapy

RICHARD G. DRUSS, M.D.

OXFORD
UNIVERSITY PRESS
2000

# OXFORD

UNIVERSITY PRESS

Oxford    New York

Athens   Auckland   Bangkok   Bogota   Bombay   Buenos Aires
Calcutta   Cape Town   Dar es Salaam   Delhi   Florence   Hong Kong
Istanbul   Karachi   Kuala Lumpur   Madras   Madrid   Melbourne
Mexico City   Nairobi   Paris   Singapore   Taipei   Tokyo   Toronto

and associated companies in
Berlin   Ibadan

Published by Oxford University Press, Inc.
198 Madison Avenue, New York, New York 10016

Oxford is a registered trademark of Oxford University Press

Library of Congress Cataloging-in-Publication Data
Druss, Richard G., 1933–
Listening to patients : relearning the art of healing in psychotherapy / Richard G. Druss.
p. ; cm.
Includes bibliographical references and index.
ISBN 0–19–513593–8
1. Psychotherapy   2. Psychotherapist and patient.   I. Title.
[DNLM: 1. Psychotherapy—methods.   2. Body Image.   3. Interpersonal Relations.
4. Mental Healing.   WM 420 D797L 2000]
RC480.D787    2000
616.89′14—dc21        00–028541

1 3 5 7 9 8 6 4 2

Printed in the United States of America
on acid-free paper

To my teachers

To my students

_____

# Acknowledgments

First and foremost I thank my wife Margery. She has been my in-house grammarian, rhetorician, and computerologist, as well as companion and soulmate, in all life's important endeavors.

Joan Bossert, Editorial Director of Oxford University Press, and I hit it off from our first telephone conversation and have been on the same beam throughout. Quite often it appeared that she knew what I was trying to say even better than I did and said it better.

Two colleagues were kind and longsuffering enough to read the entire manuscript: Dr. Paul Wender, Distinguished Professor of Psychiatry at the University of Utah, friend of my youth and adulthood; and Dr. Eve Leeman, former Chief Resident, supervisee, and current book reviewer for the *Lancet*.

Other students have read portions of this book in earlier versions and I'm grateful for their comments. They include Hilary Beattie, Edward Kenney, David Ott, Susan Swick, Maria Sullivan, and Mark Wilson.

I was blessed by having humanistic clinician-teachers in my formative years; they taught by example as well as by doctrine. Drs. Virginia Apgar in anesthesiology, Sidney Carter in neurology, Bard Cosman in surgery, Willard Gaylin in psychoanalysis, Sylvia Griffiths in pediatrics, Lawrence

Kolb in psychiatry, Helen Ranney in medicine, as well as Dr. Elizabeth Helly in mathematics all put their hand on me. I owe them a debt that can never be fully paid. But I have tried to carry on their spirit and heritage through my own teaching to students, personally and in the classroom, and with this book.

*New York City*                                          R.G.D.
*July 1999*

*The patients in this book, and their stories, have been disguised and altered to ensure their anonymity. Furthermore, two of the patients are composites.*

# Contents

LISTENING TO PATIENTS

# Introduction

I was in my first month of medical internship in Boston when I decided to go into psychiatry. Here is the story.

As was the custom, the previous interns had discharged everyone but the hopeless and cleared the decks for us newcomers. One of my three inherited patients was a woman in her seventies with advanced cirrhosis, who lay sedated, unkempt, and forgotten in a side room. She had a thick chart, but I went to see her to get my own medical history and immediately noticed her name. "Are you related to the famous Cabots (not her real name) who talk only to the Lodges?" She said she was but from the poor side of the family. Taking the history perked her up as she peppered her responses with famous Boston names and locations. She was, however, too weak to stand during my brief physical examination. I told her I would stop her nightly sleeping pill. Then I asked, "If nurse Duffy comes by later, will you let her do your hair? It needs brushing. I'll be by in the morning to check up." She smiled and nodded.

I saw her before rounds the next day. She was out of bed, sitting up in a chair. Her hair was brushed and she wore a bright red housecoat. "You look terrific, Mrs. Cabot. How about a little walk with Ms. Duffy and me at tea time?" "Yes," she said enthusiastically.

At four-thirty, she and Ms. Duffy, a student nurse, had already been practicing. Ms. Duffy handed her over to me and, light-as-a-feather, we walked the four corners of her small room. I told her that I would be back after rounds the next day and take her for a real walk, out of her room onto the main ward, the nurses station, and the visitors area. "To see the sights," she said.

The next day, she was waiting for me after rounds. She took my left arm and clung to me for dear life but managed to make it to the nurses station. "We'll show them," she whispered as we passed the Chief Resident and Service Attending. And so it went. We had a daily "stroll along the boulevard" each morning until she was strong enough to be discharged.

I was thrilled. I felt I had taken this patient left for dead, and without any new medication, had rehabilitated her. I further felt that the extra attention I gave Mrs. Cabot was due to a genuine fascination with her life and her story.

That was forty years ago. Since that time I have been practicing psychotherapy, and I can say that the thrill and excitement remain; patients' lives and stories still fascinate me, and I have not been bored for an instant. I hope to convey that excitement to the reader.

I have taught psychotherapy both in the classroom and individually as a supervisor for almost as long. This book is written for psychiatry residents, medical students, and for trainees in clinical psychology, social work, and nursing. Since it is a reader-friendly book, without an iota of jargon or psychobabble, it would be of interest as well to any educated person who would like to know more about modern dynamic psychotherapy.

I have used the anecdotal or case method of teaching with students' patients and my own. Students like to hear senior faculty present their own material, failures as well as successes. This book is filled with the examples that I have used with my students throughout the years.

I saw these patients between 1965 and 1975, setting this ten-year time limit to help preserve anonymity. Every vignette has been sufficiently disguised and altered to ensure anonymity. Choosing this decade creates an artifact: many of the patients had medical as well as psychological problems, but the principles learned apply to all patients. Also, it was my first ten years in practice, and I was a beginner at psychotherapy; my work was filled with the kind of mistakes we can all learn from now.

Although not a textbook, the chapters in this volume follow a logical and chronologic sequence—from the initial establishment of rapport with a new patient to the realization of goals at the end.

Creating rapport and taking a leisurely history were two important lessons that "Mrs. Cabot" taught me. These days I rely less and less on a long call from a colleague who is referring a new patient and more and more on what the patient can provide on his or her own. Chapter 1 will explore ways to achieve rapport and a working alliance with challenging and difficult patients.

Involving patients as joint participants in their own therapy is vital no matter what the diagnosis and no matter what the treatment: dynamic, cognitive/behavioral, or interpersonal. Patients have to be active participants in unraveling the mystery of their behavior and their suffering. Chapter 2 is devoted to enlisting the patient's participation in their treatment.

Transference is a repetition of past relationships in the patient's early history displaced onto current caretakers. Interestingly, the most intense transferences are those that people develop toward their own family doctor. Looking at this dyad in chapter 3 will enable us to understand the importance of transference phenomena in psychotherapy.

Listening to patients from different ethnic and cultural backgrounds can be a challenge for any therapist. Helping a patient resolve their intrapsychic conflicts while respecting their cultural heritage can be even more difficult. Chapter 4 covers this important topic.

In chapter 5 I address conversion reactions and body image disorders. In various guises these diagnostic entities are much more common than usually recognized; they touch on disorders of pregnancy, eating regulation, and various forms of somatization.

Supervision is a process that can enhance the psychotherapy experience for both teacher and student. Chapter 6 will discuss this unique interaction that is the modern equivalent of apprenticeship in music and the arts.

The omission of a full and free discussion of the spiritual life of our therapy patients would be as mistaken as the omission of a discussion of their sexual life, but many therapists are made vastly more uncomfortable by the former. Chapter 7 is devoted to this neglected topic.

Chapter 8 is about termination of psychotherapy. Patients and their therapists often have differing views about if and when termination should take place. This difference is usually due to a lack of communication about goals.

The final chapter is a discussion of patients who return to psychotherapy after termination, a topic often omitted in the literature on psychotherapy. In chapter 9 we will have a chance to revisit some patients presented earlier in the book.

In a world of managed care and third party accountability, we need to be efficient, doing our best and most in the least time. I try to demonstrate that therapeutic effectiveness is directly dependent on the working alliance that has been created between patient and therapist, and that the only way he or she can create that alliance is to be taught how to listen to patients. Begin with the patient, and the theory will follow. Any attempt to squeeze each patient into one's favorite theory will do credit neither to the patient nor to the theory. From this comes the principle of flexibility and imagination in conducting therapy, stressed in every chapter of this book.

Therapists must regard patients' communications as emanating from their own private, subjective world—a world we enter by invitation only. All patients should be treated with respect and a deep sense of boundaries. In this book, I demonstrate how therapy can provide a shelter and a safe place for patients to bring their experiences.

It is not enough to ask a patient to tell his or her story and then sit back stonyfaced and passive. Some patients find it hard to open up and need encouragement. Others will talk too much and need guidance to construct a coherent and useful narrative.

During my forty years in the practice of psychotherapy, I have witnessed the introduction of new psychoactive medications that are now the heart of many psychiatric treatments. But they too must be prescribed in the context of a therapeutic encounter, with trust on both sides of the aisle.

We, who have learned the skill of listening to Prozac, must now relearn the art of listening to patients.

# ONE

# Creating the Working Alliance

> What we got is a failure to communicate.
> *Cool Hand Luke*

## Success in Communication

I first met Larry when he was in the child inpatient service at Columbia. He was walking down the corridor and would have been a rather handsome boy of eleven, except for the almost continuous spasms and tics of his face and flailing movements of his arms above his head that made him look like he was walking through a large swarm of gnats. His chart indicated that his condition had deteriorated over the last six months, and he was admitted to the Psychiatric Institute for a definitive workup and treatment. Shortly before admission, he became mute so that it was almost impossible to communicate with him. The other thing that I noticed about Larry when I first met him was that he wore a short-sleeved white dress shirt with the top button buttoned; at the time, this was the stigma of the "nerd" and marked him as someone to be teased. I had a pad with me and took it and Larry to the playroom and pointed to it saying, "I suppose we'll talk with pencil and paper." He shook his head and went over to a blackboard and wrote, "I will write on the blackboard with chalk." The interesting and frustrating aspect of this form of communication was that Larry was left-handed, and his smudged writing was further obfuscated by his left wrist and elbow that would rub along, virtually erasing what he had just written. An entire hour session yielded one smudged blackboard full of brief semi-illegible replies. I will not go into all of the interesting discoveries I made regarding his history, upbringing, and emerging psychodynamics as the therapy proceeded. One discovery though that sticks in my memory was told to me by Ms. Ingram, the wonderful social worker who had been assigned to counsel Larry's parents. We spoke weekly about the case. One day she described the ambiance at the family dinner table when Larry was seven. Larry's father was a harsh disciplinarian and rewarded any spill with a "backhander" to the upper body or head. It didn't take long for us to see the meaning of Larry's arm movements, with his head ducking down and his arms jerking upward. He was like a boxer fending off blows. Ms. Ingram laughed as she surmised how Larry's involuntary spasms had greatly increased the number of stains on their pristine white tablecloth.

After about three months, Larry wrote down, unerased, "I will talk with you on Monday." I took this statement as a gift. During the time I had been working with Larry, I had grown to like this perplexing but very bright and appealing boy. Filled with anticipation, I sat down on Monday morning with him. He opened his mouth and a voice that sounded somewhere between a rusty gate hinge and a call from a distant planet squeaked to me, "My name is Larry." In my thirty years of practice this was surely one of the most moving moments. I did not ask him "why now" but responded to him directly: I offered him some water. The now vocal treatment proceeded for the rest of the year.

When I completed residency, Larry was still on the floor. He still had some of the spasms of his face, but his arms had stopped their odd movements. Perhaps, more important to him, he had chosen to unbutton his top shirt button, which showed his desire to join in with the other preteenagers.

Eve was sent to me by her internist who said I must treat this thirteen-year-old girl because all efforts at controlling her raging ulcerative colitis had failed. He and a surgeon consultant decided to give her a six-month trial of psychotherapy before she underwent a total colectomy. I protested that I did not treat children or adolescents but was persuaded to make a Hail Mary try. She was taken to my office by her parents, who brought along her hospital records. (This was some ten years after my residency and the treatment of Larry, and she was only the second child patient that I had seen.) She wore a pea jacket that she kept on during the entire session. Eve was sullen, angry at being in the office of a psychiatrist, totally uncommunicative and uncooperative. She sat staring at me, her jaw thrust out belligerently and her arms folded across her chest. How to reach her? At first I tried approaches I learned in residency training. "You don't want to be here, do you?" No answer. "You must be very angry having to see a psychiatrist against your will." No response. And on and on. She finally did answer when I asked why she thought she was here, with a terse "ulcerative colitis." And that was it for the first session. In succeeding sessions, I tried every technique that I knew of and consulted child psychiatrists for their advice, all to no avail. My own children were in their early teens and I brushed up on the current teenage television idols, magazines, and movie stars. When I mentioned them to her, the disgust on her face, if anything, increased. On a lucky day, she might give me some clipped answer as to the severity of her colitis or to the medication she was taking. Through clenched teeth she gave monosyllabic answers to what she was doing at school. This was the scope of our weekly sessions together. She never offered a spontaneous word.

Two months into the treatment, now quite desperate, I asked her what hobbies she had. She said she had none but then mentioned in an offhand way that she collected stamps. I jumped on this flicker of spontaneity and said, if she brought her stamp album I would bring mine, and we could perhaps compare and even trade. I did bring my tattered old stamp album and was surprised when she arrived with her album as well. We opened them on my desk and again I was surprised to see that she had an almost complete collection of American commemorative stamps, beautifully mounted and neatly presented. She looked up at me and saw that my admiration was genuine and flashed a tentative smile. We spent the next two sessions swapping stamps, and the patient took on the role of the teacher, advising me not to make such foolish and irresponsible trades. I must say that during this time I felt utterly fraudulent as a therapist, stealing her parents' good money. At any moment I expected the officers of the American Psychiatric Association to come storming in to my office and, like Dreyfus, have my buttons and epaulets ceremoniously removed. However, soon thereafter in the midst of stamp trades, she slowly began to talk about her condition, the frightening effect it had on her, and her absolute terror of surgery. Like the lariat Will Rogers used to introduce his act, we began each session with our stamp albums poised and ready but used them less and less as she would talk about not only her medical concerns but also her parents, sister, and schoolmates. It was at this time that I received a call from her internist that her colitis was considerably better. She was no longer taking oral steroids and was being managed on rectal steroids and asulfadine. She began to bring in dreams that dealt with her confusion between the female reproductive and gastrointestinal systems. She had just begun her menstrual periods, and there were unconscious connections between vaginal and rectal bleeding. At this time, I felt it was prudent for me to bow out of the treatment and referred her to a female social worker who could more comfortably deal with her anatomic confusion. In our final session together, she shook my hand saying "thanks." Follow-up revealed that her colitis went into permanent remission and her colon, of course, was spared.

### Breaking Through Initial Barriers to Therapy

These two young patients presented with a challenge to the psychotherapeutic process itself. One was mute and the other might as well have been. Yet we should greet these two situations as a challenge and not throw in the towel prematurely. What is interesting are the similarities in these two very different patients.

First, there was an overall ambivalence to being in psychotherapy. Every patient has a conflict between opening up and shutting down the doors of communication. Larry demonstrated his ambivalence by writing and erasing a sentence at the same moment. Eve, who never missed a session and arrived promptly, was in my office in name only, present but not voting.

Second, I needed to find something admirable in the patient to unleash my therapeutic zeal. Larry was someone I admired right away for his intelligence and wit. With Eve, it took a while, and fake attempts at fake admiration were totally unsuccessful. It wasn't until I saw her beautiful stamp album that I found something genuine and admirable in her and could build on that. Trading stamps also took her out of the subordinated patient role and she could chide and scold me for my mistakes.

Third, the barometers of my success reinforced optimism that I was getting somewhere. It is necessary for any therapist to have some indication that he or she is making headway with a patient to reinforce therapeutic optimism. It's interesting that in addition to greater communication there were signals from both patients of "opening up" by their manner of dress. Larry unbuttoned his top shirt button and looked less nerdy, less peculiar, and more ready for action. Eve unbuttoned her pea jacket and eventually took it off, which signaled to me a willingness to expose herself metaphorically as well.

And fourth, both of the cases taught me I had to be flexible in my approach to all patients. These experiences showed me, and I hope the reader, that one should not be bound by standard operating procedure. As long as one is within proper ethical guidelines and observes strict boundaries, one has to be imaginative in dealing with difficult patients. In one way or another, all patients are mute or withhold information, so our task must be to find a way to communicate. That is surely our primary job.

## Failure in Communication

I saw Mr. P. for a problem of premature ejaculation. I was in my first year of practice and this was the first well-to-do businessman that I might treat, having spent the first few months with the academic poor. When he entered my office for his first visit, he demanded, "May I use your phone?", and before I had a chance to reply was already dialing, "Hello Marilyn. It's me. I'll take all messages when I get back unless there's something urgent . . . No . . . no . . . no . . . You can expect me around 4:00 P.M. . . . Bye." He then said to me, "I just got back from Florida today." He was athletic, freshly tanned, and twenty years my senior. I asked him to tell me about himself, and he said that he had been divorced two years ago and was just finding his way in the dating scene. He explained what a great treat it was to be cavorting with all these attractive, desirable women and was going into considerable detail about his many conquests. After a time, I asked him what the problem was and he replied, "Doc, I come too quick and leave the woman unsatisfied." I asked him how long he had the "impotence problem" and regretted my question the moment I asked it. He looked at me in a fury and said, "What do you mean impotence? I'm a mass of raging hormones and I can't help it if I have such a strong libido." I tried to recover my balance by first apologizing and then explained that the Kinsey Report listed three types of male impotence: retarded ejaculation, failure of erection, and also premature ejaculation. He was too angry to hear this accurate but feeble exposition and left the session five minutes early, never to be heard from again.

During the years I was the psychiatry consultant to the plastic surgery service at Presbyterian Hospital, I received many requests for consultation from my plastic surgeon colleagues. One was a thirty-year-old single woman, Ms. Q., who wanted to have a rhinoplasty for "an overly large nose." The surgeon felt that her nose was of normal proportions, as did I when I first saw her. He hoped I would engage her in psychotherapy rather than he in plastic surgery. She spoke in a soft voice and rarely made eye contact with me. She described a rather schizoid lifestyle with few friends and little dating. All of this she blamed on her nose and felt that its gross size stood in the way of all life's successes. I found myself assuming a kind of district attorney stance and asking her a lot of questions that would distinguish an obsession with her nose from a somatic delusion. At the end of the session, I had ruled out a delusion and asked her whether she had additional questions about psychotherapy. She said that she welcomed the idea and had already been thinking about psychotherapy on her own, but felt that perhaps a different, gentler therapist might be more acceptable to her. Reluctantly, I made a good referral.

## Making the Patient Your Major Concern

With Mr. P. it's clear looking back that I was nervous anticipating my first big fee patient. It is equally clear that I responded to his bellicose and pugnacious manner with a hostile comment of my own. When I referred to his premature ejaculation as "impotence," it may have been technically correct, but it was therapeutically dreadful. With Ms. Q., I committed one of the unforgivable sins of therapy, conflict of interest. I was thinking of my career at the plastic surgery service rather than the needs of this quite treatable young woman who required explanations and reassurance about psychotherapy.

I don't think I would make these errors of judgment today. They are a product of beginner's jitters and countertransference. It pains me to write of mistakes that I would chide my students for but hope they will learn from them. Mr. P. should have been praised for his courage in coming to see a psychiatrist about a sexual problem, which in the late 1960s still had considerable stigma attached to it. Ms. Q. needed treatment and this should have been on my mind from the start. The plastic surgeons had already made up their mind about the operation, or else they would not have sent her to me.

Communication failures can result from the actual content of a dialogue, as with Mr. P., or from the tone and manner used with Ms. Q. We have no control over the so-called immediate negative transferences that emerge from the patient, where it is our bad luck to resemble some very abusive, negative figure in their background, but we should certainly try to minimize the contributions that *we* make in failing to communicate with our patients.

## A Deaf Patient

Mrs. R. was a forty-year-old married woman who had been admitted to the surgical service for an excisional biopsy of her right breast. The findings were negative for cancer, but immediately after the procedure she developed thrombophlebitis in her right leg. This condition necessitated a transfer to the medical service for anticoagulation and observation. Her right leg gave her constant pain, and she was demanding narcotics every four hours. Her physicians felt she was overreacting to a minimal problem but were handicapped in communicating with her because she was congenitally deaf, with less than 10 percent of normal hearing; she was also mute.

I was called to see her because of this acute pain problem. When I came into her room, she was seated with her right foot up on a hassock, and my very entry into her room appeared to aggravate her pain. She frowned and pulled away as I entered. We corresponded by pad and pen, but she was in pain, very angry about her leg, and barely participated in the written interview. I decided to call the Program for the Deaf at the New York State Psychiatric Institute and was given the services of a social worker who knew American Sign Language (ASL). She joined me for the second interview. One does not usually enjoy being the third party to a language interpreter and patient dyad, but I found myself entranced by the elegance and beauty of the signing between them. The patient smiled and was actively participating with the social worker, who gave me a running commentary. The patient signed that she knew that she had thrombophlebitis.

"Where did it come from?" I asked.

"It was caused by clogged veins," she replied.

"Why were the veins clogged?"

She then signed, "It was the spread of cancer cells to the leg."

Shocked by her response, I told the social worker to inform the patient that the tumor was benign and not able to spread in any way. This had been confirmed to her in writing by the surgical and medical staff, but it was not until it was signed to her *in her language*, ASL, her native tongue, that she was able to integrate and process this information. I had her chart with me and she and I read through the pathology report in the chart together, which I think sealed the bargain. Two days later I returned, and she was now dressed, smiling, with her foot no longer propped up, preparing for discharge that afternoon.

### Learning to Speak a New Language

Each patient has her or his own means through which to communicate to the outside world, often involving symptoms that communicate inner troubles in more than mere spoken language. This deaf and mute patient illustrated her pain in a dramatic way.

Once communication was instituted, the psychodynamics of this patient's exaggerated response to her pain became clear. She had made two unconscious displacements: (1) from the breast to the leg—from a scary area to a neutral one, and (2) from fear of death, about which one could do nothing, to fear of pain, about which one can be given medication. But it was impossible to arrive at this understanding and provide a liberating interpretation until the working alliance was established. In a crisis there is regression, where only one's native tongue will be understood.

The New York State Psychiatric Institute Program for the Deaf is the product of pioneer work developed by Dr. Franz Kallmann, Dr. Kenneth Altschuler and Dr. John Rainer.[1] Fast forwarding thirty years, the value of ASL with deaf medical patients was made clear once again in a 1995 *JAMA* article by David Ebert and Paul Heckerling.[2]

The problems of communication with the deaf have been depicted by Leah Hager Cohen in her wonderful book *Train Go Sorry: Inside a Deaf World*. She grew up in the Lexington School for the Deaf, where she was the daughter of the director and American Sign Language became her second language. Cohen in 1994 advises that

> for more than a century, doctors and educators had advised parents not to allow their deaf children to learn sign language. . . . In spite of their good intentions, they ended up withholding from their children the one language that *could* be acquired visually. . . . Because deaf children do not acquire an aural spoken language naturally, they must be taught every minute element that hearing children absorb effortlessly, and they were sent to school with no language system at all.[3]

Oliver Sacks, in *Seeing Voices: A Journey into the World of the Deaf*, used his particular descriptive skills to depict sign language itself in detail, and he also had a sense of awe and respect for its subtlety and beauty. Sacks described the battles for "deaf power" at Gallaudet University, the only liberal arts college for the deaf in the world and the hub of the world's deaf community. But in its first 124 years, it had never had a deaf president. These are Sacks's words:

> But almost at once I was to be made aware of another mention, another world of considerations, not biological

but cultural. Many of the deaf people I met acquired good language of an entirely different sort, a language that served not only the powers of thought but served as a medium of rich community and culture. . . . While I never forgot the medical status of the deaf, I now had to see them in a new ethnic light, as a people, with a language sensibility and culture of their own.[4]

But probably the most poignant and familiar example is the film *Children of a Lesser God,* where a deaf woman prefers the elegance of ASL to some garbled, guttural version of English and ultimately refuses to speak at all.[5]

I have seen performances of the National School for the Deaf and there *is* a special beauty in sign language that is somewhere between language and ballet. It is not unlike Chinese art that has regarded calligraphy, the actual language characters, as not only worthy of a master's art but also the highest form of the visual arts.

I have not had the opportunity to treat or consult with a deaf patient since, but I hope I have learned that the basis for the working alliance with any patient is respect for differences and admiration for the courage with which people have attempted to overcome their limitations and the hand that they were dealt at birth.

## *Nurturing the Working Alliance*

The concept of the working alliance has been written about before. Psychoanalysts and therapists of every stripe have described the patient-therapist relationship outside the transference in various terms: the "therapeutic alliance,"[6] "the mature transference,"[7] and "the working alliance."[8] Ralph Greenson and Milton Wexler defined the working alliance as "the non-neurotic, rational, reasonable rapport that the patient has with his analyst and which enables him to work purposefully in the analytic situation." Joseph Sandler and his associates give a nice review of the subject to date and state that the concept draws upon what Erikson has called "basic trust": an attitude in people which is based on the infants' experiences of security in the first months of life. The reestablishment of a state of trust has been found to be a necessary requirement in patients who have experienced severe emotional depravation as children.[9]

Cognitive therapy, as exemplified by Aaron Beck and his colleagues, discusses "the therapeutic relationship." They describe the characteristics of the therapist that help produce the relationship: warmth and acceptance, accurate empathy, honesty and genuineness. They feel the therapeutic relationship is based on rapport, "the harmonious accord between people." They speak of the necessity for the therapist to enter the patient's subjective world and "to try it on." Part of the artistry of cognitive therapy also involves instilling a sense of adventure inherent in the task.[10]

Interpersonal psychotherapy (IPT) was developed by Gerald Klerman and Myrna Weissman as a time-limited, weekly treatment for ambulatory, nonpsychotic, depressed patients. IPT focuses on the patients' present interpersonal environment and is less concerned with revisiting the home of origin. The therapist is active, not passive; she is the patient's advocate, not neutral; she does not promote the therapeutic relationship as a transference experience but keeps it bound in reality. The goals are rapid symptom reduction and the facilitation of interpersonal success. Quick establishment of a sound working alliance is a prerequisite for any time-limited therapy and for IPT in particular.[11]

It seems clear to me that whether the treatment be a dynamic therapy, a cognitive therapy, or an interpersonal therapy, a positive, comfortable working alliance must precede all else. Only someone who is truly a madman would be shouting out their troubles to the world on a soapbox. Most people need to trust their listener and feel that they are in "a safe place" to quote Lesten Havens.[12] I am reminded of the apocryphal story of a young psychiatrist who failed his board exams when he told the examiner that there was no mental status because the patient was mute.

When I am confronted with a patient from an unusual background or unfamiliar place, I will read up on it and try and get inside the subjective life of my patient as quickly as I can. If the person is taking medication, whether it be psychotropic medication or medication for an illness, I am particularly interested in its effects, its side effects, and possible drug interactions.

Unless the patient is in the midst of an acute crisis, I try to begin my investigation with a history. We spend time on the patient's autobiography, getting sketches about parents and upbringing. Not only does this history provide a grounding for further information to follow, but also the experience of discussing the patient's own background is one of the most effective ways of beginning communication and developing rapport. I do not find this task an onerous one: on the contrary, we should love biography. Conducting psychotherapy gives the psychiatrist the chance to live many lives as well as his own.

When the patient finds it difficult to tell his or her story, we comfortably invoke the concept of resistance. And certain kinds of information that deal with shameful, guilt-ridden and, to them, prohibited acts and thoughts will produce resistance. But we would be remiss if we conceived of patients' difficulties in opening up to the therapist as solely the product of resistance. Let us take a step back and look at the idiosyncrasies, peculiarities, and uniqueness of the patient-therapist relationship. It is not equal. It should not be equal.

The patient exposes more than the therapist. Many patients feel that the entire relationship is odd and respond to this unfamiliarity with anxiety and apprehension. We don't answer questions initially because hopefully in time we will both find the meaning of the question more interesting than the reply. One should explain that the reason it is one-sided and focused on the patient is to facilitate communication without therapist interference or intrusion or bias. Opportunities for the patient's questions, concerns, and doubts should be made available at the end of each early session and answered as directly as possible.

Residents and other trainees should beware of imitating the great virtuoso interviewers who make rounds on their patients. Often they do such a thorough and careful dissection of the patient that they leave the trainee with the task of putting humpty-dumpty together again. It is a mistake to try to emulate this virtuosity in practice. "The Use of Force" is a well-known story by William Carlos Williams.[13] In it, Williams, a young pediatrician, forces open the mouth of a young child to rule out diphtheria in the child's throat. This is an emergency, and the information needs to be forcibly unearthed in spite of the fierce and rapacious struggle between them. He makes his diagnosis, but we can surmise that the patient will dread future encounters with a physician.

I regard the *Diagnostic and Statistical Manual*[14] as one of the most valuable and heuristic documents in psychiatry. It has made communication among therapists possible by standardizing the criteria of psychiatric diagnoses. But as therapists we are also interested in what is different in people and not only in what is the same. And the DSM was not designed to encompass the uniqueness and individuality of people's lives. For example, twenty consecutive patients suffering from generalized anxiety disorder will be very different people. Yes, both Haydn and Bartok wrote string quartets for the same instruments, in the same sonata form and structure, but they sound and are very different creations.

The appreciation of these precious differences is only possible in a psychotherapeutic encounter, where there is a trusting storyteller and an appreciative, understanding listener, both eager to communicate.

TWO

# The Initial Sessions

## *Setting the Course*

---

Before any psychotherapy can be properly launched, there are arrangements to be made.

First, the patient must be allotted a consistent time slot, whether it is every fourth week or four times a week. The therapist should be on time. I do not see two patients back-to-back, that is, without a break; time would have to be taken from one patient or the other. I feel an interval of ten minutes gives me full time to shift gears, answer any telephone messages, and do my own ablutions.

Second, the therapist must pledge total confidentiality. And this pledge must be for real: no name dropping, no gossip, no pillow talk. Except for matters of life and death, nothing leaves the office.

Third, the patient and therapist must settle on a fee that is comfortable to both.

When all the above have been accomplished, the therapist can begin to enlist the help of the patient in the therapeutic journey. It is to this important task that I wish to devote the chapter.

I received a call from Mr. G., the successful manager of a mutual fund, requesting an appointment. He said he didn't feel he needed to see me, but his exasperated wife had demanded "get therapy or get lost." He was thirty-nine, married for fifteen years, loved his wife and two little sons, and would do anything for them, even therapy. So with difficulty we were able to set up a two-hour appointment for Friday afternoon.

He arrived late, carrying two enormous briefcases filled with his weekend's supply of financial homework. He looked like an ex-football player who had stopped working out: twenty pounds overweight, puffing, with plethoric facies. His wife's biggest complaint was that he worked so hard that she and the boys, seven and nine, felt completely neglected. She said even when he was around he was chronically irritable and preoccupied. He disputed none of this, citing the demands of his new position, and anyway it would only be a year at most until things settled. "It's like your year of internship Dr. Druss, one very tough year," and he felt his wife should accommodate for this short period of time. Would I like to see her? I said, "Not now. Let's get to know you and hear your autobiography right from the start."

He was born in Dellwood, Wisconsin, dairy country, and his father was a hard-working farmer. He had a sister two years his junior who still maintained the old family home. His own milestones were normal and he did especially well in school. I was transcribing all this historical data in detail when he dropped, "Then in the first grade my father suddenly died." "My goodness," I said, "What did he die from?" You know, I can't remember. "How did your mother take it? How did you all manage?" He thought awhile and said, "I can't recall that either, but a year later my mother died." I put my pen down. "What did *she* die from?" I really don't know. "You were seven and your sister was five, who raised you after that?" My grandparents, Mommy and Poppy, took the two of us in. It was difficult. They were on in years and I remember being teased at school that my father had grey hair and false teeth. "No idea at all how your parents died?" No. "Well, we have a mystery to solve." We set up an appointment for next Tuesday and he left.

He arrived promptly at 5:00 P.M. for Tuesday's appointment. Instead of his huge briefcases, he had only a slim attaché case on his lap. "When I got home Friday evening, I was upset and called my sister in Dellwood. I told her I'd be flying out the next day. I flew to Milwaukee and drove the hour to our old house. Things felt unreal. I had lunch with Frieda for the first time in years. Then after lunch I went up to the attic; I was drawn to my father's desk. It's strange but I was drawn to the middle drawer on the left. I don't know what I was looking for, and I don't recall ever looking in that desk before. But there in that drawer were old official documents. At the bottom of the pile were the death certificates of my folks. Do you want to see them?"

"I sure do," I said. He reached into the attaché case on his lap and withdrew two handwritten yellowed pages. The first, of his father, listed myocardial infarction as the immediate cause of death. The second, of his mother, listed cerebral hemorrhage. But both had chronic hypertensive vascular disease as underlying causes of death. "High blood pressure," I said. "You know, Dr. Druss, my wife has been nagging me to see a therapist for years—Why now?", he said to me. "Why now, indeed?" I asked, "What do you think?"

He thought for a long while. "Well, last month our company initiated annual physical examinations for all executives. The doctor said that I had bad high blood pressure and with my smoking and obesity I was heading for an early coronary." At this point he stopped talking, his eyes welled up and he said, "I don't want to do to my own kids what my father did to me, so I'm very determined."

We set up regular appointments twice a week. He was as good as his word and never missed a session for three years.

The treatment was largely psychodynamic, but we gave full attention to changes in lifestyle in the present day. He consulted a nutritionist and joined Smoke Enders®. He and his wife began to run together Saturday and Sunday mornings before the boys got up, which had romantic dividends as well as metabolic ones.

As his elaborate politeness wore off, he would level scathing philippics against me and the medical profession as a whole. (Much of this anger originated with repressed feelings toward medicine for allowing his parents to die so young, leaving him an orphan.) He did very well. Although he still worked very hard for long hours, he stopped taking his work home with him and retired his two massive briefcases. His disposition improved considerably, and he ended therapy leaner and less mean.

In the previous chapter I spoke of the need to begin each therapy by eliciting the patient's history. I had no idea where the history would take us or that it would yield such striking and dramatic dividends. But I had made a number of assumptions. First, if a patient had gotten himself to my office somehow, he belonged there, and it was my job to find out why. Also, I figured we could get his wife's input later on if the history did not lead to something productive. As I said before, most patients do not object to giving a thorough autobiographical narration. It serves to orient us chronologically and plants the seed that present problems are rooted in the past. Sidney Tarachow in his 1963 text makes the point that the initial sessions should be devoted to a structured and careful inquiry of a new patient's history.[1] Brian Bird also stresses that getting to know the whole patient and the patient's unique background is a necessary prelude to understanding his current plight.[2]

We have seen that with Mr. G. it was the elicitation of his history that propelled and motivated him to begin psychotherapy. Labeling the material as a "mystery" would hopefully pique his curiosity about his motivation; he was someone whose successful work involved financial puzzle solving and I just had to hitch that motivation and skill to self-discovery. The trip to Dellwood to begin intrapsychic detective work prognosticated well, and the results further intrigued him—and me.

The question, "Why now?" that we both asked was crucial. His wife had been urging him to begin therapy for years, but it was the executive physical examination with the discovery of hypertension that had been the acute precipitant. This finding, coupled with my question "What did your parents die from?", motivated him to make this dramatic trip back to Dellwood. He must have seen the death certificates years before and repressed the diagnoses. But the force of that repressed memory led him back to his home of origin, back to the attic, and back to the middle drawer of his father's old desk.

Mr. G. had been abandoned in his childhood by both parents. He felt he could only rely on himself as a sure thing. Yet he was a loved person, by his sister, his grandmother, and his childhood sweetheart who later became his wife. His life was dominated by a sense of purpose.

The psychotherapy setting reshuffled the cards. He had a deep-seated yearning for a father, a father to identify with, and one that was different from the demanding father whom he remembers when he was five years old. And a father to fight with, harmlessly, as do all sons in their adolescence. And a father he could respect who paid attention to measurable items like exercise, weight, blood pressure. And a father who would not abandon him in times of difficulty. He found these qualities in therapy and flourished.

Mr. H. was always complaining. He was the CEO of a small company that manufactured women's clothes. He was fifty-two, in excellent health, married to a loving wife, and the father of two spritely teenage girls. Along with his two brothers, he had inherited the family business from his father and being the eldest, he was the boss. He had been a mathematics major in college, but at the insistence of his overbearing father he took classes in accounting and was groomed to manage the business.

"I don't have the personality for it," he told me in our first session. "How can I predict women's hemlines a year in advance?" "The garment worker's union wants higher wages and I'm not a negotiator." "Each of my brothers is stupider than the other, and all the responsibility for the business falls on my shoulders." One weekend after another was spoiled largely due to his preoccupation with work. The reason he decided on initiating therapy now was that he could not participate in his beloved elder daughter's sweet sixteen party. Although not overtly depressed, I noticed that he complained about everything in an unending litany: filthy streets, crowded subways, and bad weather. Our sessions were one series of complaints after another.

Finally, in our tenth session, I asked him, "Mr. H., in this miserable week of yours is there nothing that gives you joy?" He stopped in his tracks, paused a bit, and then blushed with embarrassment. (What lascivious secret was he about to confess?) "Well," he said hesitatingly, "There is. Two hours, from ten to twelve each Sunday, I teach Bible class at a small Yeshiva in the Bronx near where I grew up." His whole countenance changed as he described sitting on a little chair telling the seven-year-old boys about Noah, Abraham, Joseph, and Moses. He was smiling for the first time. "Quite something," I said as the session ended.

He came in excited the next time. "I have a plan," he said. Mr. H. described the discussion he had initiated with an old friend on the business faculty of a nearby college. "He said I can begin teaching management as an adjunct. It will add two hours to my day on Tuesday and Thursday evenings. Terrible idea, right Dr. Druss?"

"You won't know until you try," I responded.

He began teaching the next month, and he described how on Tuesday and Thursday nights, rather than feeling more exhausted, he felt "energized," and walked with a lighter step. On Monday, Wednesday, and Friday he came home and greeted his family with his usual splenetic visage.

He was animated in our discussions and full of ideas and schemes. Could I teach full time? That would be heaven, but it would mean a huge cut in income. The students love me and need to hear the voice of experience. One day he told me that his wife wanted to see me about this potential major change in his life. Please talk to her Dr. Druss.

Mrs. H. came to see me. "Is Morris going through some midlife crisis and this just some temporary phase?" She described the improved quality of life for her and the girls. "Do you support this change?" I asked. "Of course I do. I have never seen Morris so happy—it's worth more than all the money in the world."

Before the year was out Mr. H. had sold his controlling share of the business to his two brothers for a tidy sum. That, plus his professional salary, plus a little belt tightening, was sufficient. He left therapy a happy man.

The reader will note that during the first ten initial sessions, I made only one significant intervention: "Is there nothing that gives you joy?" This was first of all a diagnostic question: Was Mr. H. joyless because he was chronically dysthymic or, as I had hoped, were there hidden joys that he was ashamed to remember? Here was a mystery. He felt his father surely and me, via a paternal transference, would not approve of an unmanly activity like telling Bible stories to little Yeshiva boys. Second, my question was a demand to Mr. H.—*you must come up with the answer*—I don't know it. (It was not unlike Freud pressing the forehead of his early analytic patients to squeeze out the embarrassing truth that was hidden and repressed.) The idea that he should expand this weekly experience and teach business to adults was his. The idea that he should sell his share in the hated business and teach full time was also his. The clothing business had always been his father's dream and even when he became CEO, it was never his own. We discussed this equation, business = father, often during therapy, which both tormented him and made his life miserable. Nevertheless these insights of therapy freed him to make the kind of decisions that he hadn't made when he graduated college. Psychotherapy gave Mr. H. a second chance.

## Psychotherapy Is a Mutual Enterprise

Most therapists have emphasized, and rightly so, the early affective engagement of a new patient. I feel that engaging the patient intellectually is equally as important. Patients must be disabused of the idea that they can just come in, pour out their feelings, and that magically the therapist will cure them. Psychotherapy is a two-person task and two-person adventure. I often illustrate this point to the patient with the explanation that we will be taking a trip down the middle fork of the Salmon River in a two-person raft, with them in the bow and me in the stern. I may know more about psychotherapy, but they know much more about themselves. Together we can navigate a journey that neither of us could accomplish alone. I tell them that the expedition will be one of discovery, sometimes exhilarating, sometimes frustrating, even dangerous, and the end will not now be in sight.

Frieda Fromm-Reichmann, in her *Principles of Intensive Psychotherapy*, states, "In order to start out right the psychiatrist should remember that intensive psychotherapy is a mutual enterprise, a mutual adventure."[3] I fully agree with this.

As I mentioned in chapter 1, Ralph Greenson stresses the working alliance, which he feels, along with the neurotic suffering of the patient, provides the incentive for the patient to participate in his or her own therapy.[4] He feels that a patient's neurotic suffering: the guilt, fears, and worries that trouble him, originate in his "experiencing ego," while the part of the patient that can recognize this suffering and describe it to the therapist is the "observing ego." Having dysphoric feelings in the presence of a benign therapist is only half the task. Describing them to the therapist in a way that both can begin to understand is the other half.

Initially, the therapist must serve as a guide in explaining the unique nature and the many strange and artificial rules of psychotherapy. I feel some brief pedagogy is necessary. For example, a patient was asked by Greenson in the first session, "What is your full name?" The patient replied, "George Washington." "Why in the world did you say that?", asked Greenson. "Because that is what came to mind," said the patient! This is a misunderstanding of free association. It is not useful; it will not go anywhere. An early patient of mine, when instructed to "free associate," began to read the titles of the books on my shelf. This too will not take us very far down the Salmon River.

One of the great virtues of Glenn Gabbard's text is that it adheres to the DSM-IV diagnostic categories and language that trainees are familiar with, rather than a purely psychoanalytic framework that may be quite alien to them.

It remains totally psychodynamic, however. He stresses the differences between the medical interview and the psychotherapeutic interview with the latter engaging the new patient as an active collaborator in an exploratory process.[5]

These two early patients of mine illustrate that curiosity about themselves, planted in the first few sessions, will bear fruit later on. Both examples were exceptional and high-functioning men. Mr. G. was an economic analyst used to problem solving. Mr. H. was the only person I have met who could regularly solve the mathematics teasers in the back of *Scientific American* magazine.

Nonetheless, all patients must be challenged to use their observing ego as well as their experiencing ego. As seen above, it need not lead to an intellectualized therapeutic process.

The task of the initial sessions was to begin to engage the patient emotionally *and* intellectually in our joint expedition.

THREE

# Positive Transferences in Psychotherapy

Evocation of transference is not the exclusive province of psychotherapy. On the contrary, responses to other caregivers may demonstrate the power of transference phenomena even more dramatically. The main difference is that we in psychotherapy examine and use the transference data; non-psychiatric physicians see transference as a pleasant or irritating by-product of his or her work.

Leo Stone in *The Psychoanalytic Situation*[1] comments on the origins of psychoanalysis in medicine and psychiatry. He feels that analysis must always address itself to the suffering of the patient and not merely be an investigative or an educational experience. This fact, he writes, is based ultimately on the phenomenon of transference that originates in any suffering human being. "The medical relationship, of all specific and structured relationships between adults, to the extent that its latent psychic content becomes available, is, in my opinion, a uniquely strategic starting place for the development of a profound understanding of basic and general human psychological reactions." How much more the case for the patient's encounters with his physicians in life and death matters.

I will use "transference" as Glenn Gabbard defines it: "a repetition of past relationships in the patient's own history displaced onto current caretakers."[2] Because it follows from the theme of collaboration in psychotherapy developed in the first two chapters, I will focus on positive transferences and their chronologic development.

Willard Gaylin stated that an infant is a fetus who is born one year prematurely. No species is so helpless and so dependent at birth.[3] During the first year the infant feels a variety of severe discomforts: first, in the gastrointestinal tract with regular bouts of hunger; occasional colic and constipation as well may arise causing pain. Second are unpleasant sensations from the skin and body surface; pain and cold in particular. Third, there is a generalized neuromuscular-autonomic irritability that can overwhelm the newborn with an anxiety that is bodywide. We can only guess at the ideational content, if any, in the mind of this miserable-looking baby.

The initial caretaker, usually the mother, but it can be any male or female caretaker, serves as best as possible to lessen these primitive discomforts. She nurses the infant, alleviating the pain of its hunger or thirst. She warms it and ensures that sharp objects are not pressing against its tender skin. And she holds it close, assuaging the violence of its internal neuromuscular discharges. John Bowlby has demonstrated the failure-to-thrive syndrome so prevalent in infants who are not held or deprived of physical contact on a regular basis.[4]

Few adult patients regress to that level of primitive bodily need. One sees this level of regression in those terminally ill with AIDS or cancer, those poststroke patients with compromised mental functioning, or even perhaps someone in the midst of a severe panic attack. Internal stimuli overwhelm their compromised ego, and they are responsive and helped only by physical ministrations and calmative medications, the milk of adulthood; no words will help. The transference to the physician, often totally unconscious, is to that initial healer and caregiver who nourishes, relieves pain, and lays on hands of comfort. Much of this function is now taken up by other caregivers, such as nurses and physical therapists. (Mr. Y. in chapter 5 manifests this phenomenon.) But the unconscious hope is that the physician will somehow use these nonverbal techniques that will lovingly lessen the pain and relieve the primitive discomforts.

The second positive transference harkens back to a later phase, when the child is venturing forth; he is encountering other children, perhaps beginning nursery school. Now he may suffer physical and verbal insults. He falls. He cannot button a jacket or tie a shoe. He experiences failures at school and the everyday attacks of his classmates. He returns home with a skinned knee or wounded pride. The parent, usually the good mother, will listen. Listening to the story is often all that is necessary. According to Stanley Jackson in an article on the "listening healer," the good listener is the best physician for those who are ill in thought or feeling. Attentive listening can turn an inchoate litany of discomforts into a gradually coherent story of distress and discomfort. He cites William Osler who is alleged to have said, "Listen to the patient; he is telling you the diagnosis." Jackson adds that while the emphasis on looking is still important in gathering and appraising medical data, at times it can overwhelm the equally important need for an attentive and concerned listener.[5]

A stanza from the poet Bialik illustrates the idealized figure of the comforting listener:[6]

> And should you wish to see and know
> Their Mother, faithful, loving, kind,
> Who gathered all the burning tears
> Of her bespattered, helpless sons,

And when to her warm bosom they came
She tenderly wiped off their tears
And sheltered them, and shielded them
And lulled them in her lap to sleep.

The mother also has magical cures: the kiss to make the pain go away; the aspirin to lower the fever; the cough syrup. (A current commercial for Robitussin on TV features cough medicines ordered by "Dr. Mom.") Also, the mother offers reassurance—the complaint isn't so serious—self-esteem can be salvaged—tomorrow is another day. She gives perspective and reality testing.

The family doctor at his best embodies this transferential healing power. He first listens to the chief complaint which seems so worrisome. He hears it out and can then provide the reassurance of experience and reality. The acne will get better; there is a medication for the arthritis; the stomach pain at 4:00 A.M. is not cancer after all. There is a magical transference to the physician who can listen without judgment and offer a way of relief that not only reassures but also augments self-esteem. Every patient unconsciously wishes for a "Dr. Mom" of the cough syrup ads, who is the legendary "family doctor who makes house calls" from the past. Perhaps he did exist as depicted, but it is more likely a transference yearning from one's childhood.

The third transference figure originates in the child's latency period. It is usually to the father as a man of action: the father who can fix a flat tire, remove a splinter, repair a broken toy. The soldier sleeps at night knowing that a brave leader will be taking them into battle the next morning. In a famous scene from Shakespeare's *Henry the Fifth* of the night before the battle of Agincourt, King Henry is walking among his nervous troops making his presence known.

The physician or surgeon will suture a wound or lance a boil. He asks that we endure some pain in the procedure, and we gamely follow him because we know he treats us fairly and that the pain will pass. He appeals to our heroism. This is a more mature transference. It contains the kind of worship that the latency child has for sports heroes, and sports heroes have for their coaches. One puts one's fears and self-centered goals aside for a coach like Vince Lombardi, wrote the lineman Jerry Kramer of the 1967 Green Bay Packers in *Instant Replay*.[7] Also, the coach is not a quitter, will not abandon us on a bad day, and like his cousin the drill sergeant of basic training, can turn boys into men. As we noted previously, identification plays as big a role as transference in development of courage for, unlike the coach or drill sergeant, the physician must not convey the counterpart of Coach Lombardi's equally famous words, "winning is everything." Not all medical battles can be won. And the hope for the good father is for the man who will also be there when one is relegated to the bench. It is fundamentally an idealized figure who can fix things. This transference allows the patient to endure many uncomfortable procedures and accept them stoically.

A fourth transference is a sublimated idealizing crush on the physician or nurse and is quite a common phenomenon. The doctor is overidealized because he or she accepts the patient's lesions and deformities. Betty Rollin writes of her breast surgeon in *First You Cry:*

Why did I lust for my dear elderly surgeon? Because during those weeks he was the only man with whom I felt beautiful. He was used to the sight of severed breasts. And in this land of one-breasted women, mostly, I assumed, older and saggier than me—I felt like a goddess. And the only man who made me feel that (not because of anything he did of course, only because of my madness), was old walleyed Dr. Singerman. Meanwhile, for my poor husband, I remained dry as a gourd.[8]

It has been said that no one will ever feel as safe, loved, and secure again as the six-year-old child walking with its little hand in its father's big one: My daddy is the smartest, strongest, biggest man in the world. It is the transference from that developmental phase that affects some individuals with illness. The father comes home cranky and filled with the cares of the world, but she observes how his eyes light up with pleasure when she enters the room and the strength of his embrace when she runs to him. (See the case of Mrs. J. in chapter 6.)

The sick patient may respond to the physician that same way. He seems wise, all-powerful, unconditionally accepting. In childhood, it is a short phase, too short both for child and parent; but it may be reevoked for the patient in times of illness.

I treated one woman of thirty who still saw her pediatrician for her medical care. She had been raised fatherless and he was as close to a father as she ever had. Also, she could remain a protected child in this relationship.

Ethel Person, in her book, *Dreams of Love and Fateful Encounters,* devotes a chapter to transference love. She begins by saying that the less power one has or feels, the stronger the transference will be. She describes how aging and sick men often fall in love with their nurses, citing such examples as Joseph Heller and Thomas Merton. The adult's original sense of omnipotence is whittled away gradually by chronic illness. One hope of restoration is based on a restored sense of acceptance of her physical self. Another is through the idealization of "the other," often a physician. One aspect of transference love, she suggests, is motivated by weakness, need, and illness.[9]

The final form of transference that I will discuss is derived from late adolescence and is the least primitive. The positive elements can be seen in a college student, eager to learn, questioning, and skeptical. Like some new recruits in the Peace Corps, they are passionate about ideas and ideals and cooperative with their leader. In any adolescent there is a potential for negative responses to authority that manifest themselves in behavior that is risk-seeking and defiant.

I recall one patient, a man in his fifties, who remarked to me during the course of a psychoanalytic psychotherapy that he was being treated for a serum cholesterol of 250. He was under the care of a physician in his eighties who had been giving him a series of cholesterol-lowering agents all of which produced unpleasant side effects. In response to my enquiry, he indicated that this venerable physician had been his parents' beloved doctor, and that the patient regarded his word as law. We were, at the time, dealing with issues of autonomy and separation from the tenets of his deceased parents, and he raised the issue of whether he dared to see a consulting cardiologist who would be a contemporary. He did, and not only was almost instant rapport achieved, but also the two of them worked out a program of diet and exercise that not only were without side effects, but also improved his sense of well-being as it normalized his cholesterol. In this case the medical and psychological goals went hand in hand.

I believe that the personality and manner of the physician are major variables that determine which of these two sides of the adolescent coin will emerge. The paternalistic model of the doctor-patient relationship is particularly unsuccessful with these individuals, whether they be eighteen or seventy-eight. Paternalism may lead to "noncompliance" with any long-term treatment regimen. Many of these adolescent transferences may be shifted to the positive valence by the deliberative model described by Linda and Ezekiel Emanuel. "In the deliberative model, the physician acts as a teacher or friend, engaging the patient in a dialogue on what course of action will be best."[10]

Lewis Thomas, recalled making house calls with his physician-father and describes the lower expectations of patients in the 1930s before the age of antibiotics.[11] The role of the physician was not to cure but to wisely proclaim a diagnosis. His task was to stay with the patient until the crisis passed, offering whatever comfort he could. Before 1930, there were about ten drugs in the doctor's metaphoric black bag rather than the ten thousand available today, and expectations were low. Cures, when they came, were the will of God. "For of the Most High commeth healing" is still the motto over the entrance to the Presbyterian Hospital in New York City. Thomas goes on to say that physicians achieved little wealth, gave much time, and were honored because of this, but not idealized.

The patient-physician relationship is regarded as a central focus of medicine. As Richard Glass suggests, it is being discussed much more now but largely in terms of the changing economics of medical care. Glass quotes Frances Peabody who wrote seventy years ago that a too narrow focus on the biology of disease can inhibit the personal relationship with the patient that would enhance effective diagnosis and treatment.[12]

Beyond economics and beyond the new technology is a recognition of what psychodynamics can teach us about what the patient brings to this fateful encounter. The patient, under the thrall of illness, regresses and transferences emerge. Understanding this can enable the physician to facilitate what Robert Crenshaw and his colleagues call the "moral enterprise grounded in a covenant of trust."[13]

# FOUR

# Conflict, Personality, and Culture in Psychotherapy

Patients bring three entities with them to psychotherapy: their various internal conflicts, their personality, and their cultural heritage. This division is an artificial one, but it may be useful to examine each of them separately in order to see patients from a broader humanistic viewpoint.

The psychologic conflict is between two intrapsychic forces, and although it is a battle that is entirely unconscious, it can be a vicious and enervating one. The two forces are a wish, often a forbidden sexual or aggressive one, and the prohibitions against the realization of that wish.

Personality refers to the accustomed and habitual ways individuals deal with the world. (Character and temperament are two terms with similar connotations.) One's personality is a product of his biologic inheritance, his early upbringing, and his familiar ways of resolving intrapsychic conflict. An individual's temperament is remarkably consistent over his or her lifetime, from childhood through adulthood.[1]

A person's cultural heritage is the totality of socially transmitted behavior patterns, arts, belief systems, institutions, and all other products of human work and thought.

I will discuss Ms. E. and Dr. F., two patients where these three axes transected very dramatically. They both presented with conversion disorders. Formerly called "conversion hysteria," a patient with conversion disorder manifests physical symptoms or defects that suggest a neurological disease. I will offer a few more definitions before we proceed with their case histories.

According to psychoanalytic theory, conversion is caused by the repression of an unconscious conflict and the conversion of its anxiety into a physical symptom.[2]

Primary gain is the desire to keep the unpleasant intrapsychic conflict repressed and out of awareness.

But there is also secondary gain which refers to the benefits that accrue to people as a result of their being sick. A principle of military psychiatry derived from experiences with conversion symptoms in World War II was to treat patients as quickly as possible and close to the site of injury.[3] This program was intended to reduce the accumulation of secondary gain; pride and identification with the unit also helped in recovery.

Third, abreaction is a process by which repressed material, especially a painful experience, is quickly brought into consciousness. In the process, the patient not only recalls but also relives the experience. Insight usually results from the process. Abreaction could be analogized to lancing a boil, painful for the moment but followed by relief and hopefully healing.

Some years ago I received an apologetic call from the emergency room resident asking whether I would come in to see Ms. E., a high school sophomore. It was a Sunday morning and she had been deaf and totally paralyzed from the waist down since Friday night. She had been raised in a Catholic school in Puerto Rico and had come to New York with her family two years previously. The neurologic exam was negative.

When I arrived at the E.R. in my white coat, I was implored by three generations of the patient's family all talking simultaneously. The two residents and I wheeled the girl into a quiet room and spent the next five hours with her. She was wearing Snoopy pajamas, holding a stuffed animal, and she looked angelic.

"I'm glad you can read lips so we can talk to each other," I began prayerfully. She replied she could talk but was very nervous. I ordered a few 15 milligram tablets of phenobarbital and gave her the first. "Is that better?" "Yes."

"Why don't we start with Friday and go through the whole day hour by hour. Can you do that?" "Oh yes."

"I awoke at seven," she began, "and had breakfast."

"What did you have?"

"Orange juice and cereal."

"What kind of cereal" I asked, intent on her missing no detail.

"Cheerios."

"Cheerios?"

"Yes, Cheerios."

"What then?"

"Maria, my best friend, came by."

"Yes?"

"Then Maria and I walked to school and had first period."

"What was that?" I was calming but boringly monotonous. "Arithmetic."

"What are you doing in arithmetic?"

"Geometry. Then I had Latin." She was talking more easily.

"Who are you reading in Latin?"

"Caesar."

"Who is Caesar writing about, Vercingetorix?"

She smiled. "Did you like Latin too?"

"Oh, yes" I said. "What was the next class."

She began to look uncomfortable. "It's hard to remember."

I gave her a third phenobarbital tablet. "We had gym."

I asked her, "What happened there?"

She described the uneventful girls basketball game and then she became more restless as she described dawdling in the girls locker room. With her back to the line of lockers, she heard the faint voices of two popular girls laughing about the Friday night dance. They were having a contest as to who would be the first to produce an erection in their boyfriend by dancing close. The more she tried to listen the fainter their voices became. Then when she tried to stand her leg buckled under her and she collapsed. The school nurse was called and she was taken home. Throughout Saturday her legs weakened further until she could no longer use them.

By now she was whimpering and clutching her stuffed animal. "That was very scary," she told me.

"Yes, it was," I said, and tentatively added, "Also exciting maybe?"

She looked up at me and asked, "Do you think I'll be better enough to go to next month's dance?"

"What do you think?"

"Well, maybe. If I do, I don't have to act the way those other girls do."

I smiled. "Good for you! You could go and do just what's right for you."

With this she relaxed considerably and put aside the stuffed animal. I then said, "Maybe your toes have some movement in them already." She looked at her legs intently. Her toes began to wiggle. "Terrific," I said. Slowly over the next hour she began to move the rest of her legs. Then with a big smile on her face and holding the shoulders of the two residents for support, she walked slowly into the main E.R. Other than the fact that her right leg was still a bit weak, she was restored.

Her family rushed over. As I walked by they murmured reverently and kissed the fringes of my garments.

I am compressing five dramatic hours into a few sentences, but it was clear that Ms. E. fulfilled the DSM-IV criteria for conversion reaction.[4] The intrapsychic conflict was between her wish to hear the exciting discussion about boys and sexuality and her inner prohibition against it; the desire to stay in the locker room and to run from it. Her paralysis also made it impossible for her to attend the evening dance and permitted her to avoid the issue of boy-girl interaction. Her use of the stuffed animal was also a flight into childhood—at first clutching it, then putting it aside as she would face adult womanhood.

I was pleased that she could "read lips" and eventually could "hear" me. Not only did it make the interview easier but also her high level of suggestibility prognosticated well. The treatment was a mixture of hypnosuggestion, abreaction, and sedation, jerry-built for the emergency room setting. The brief two-day duration of symptoms prevented the accumulation of secondary gain.

The emergency room experience with Ms. E. was a five-hour abreaction. She did not need the "truth serum" (amobarbital) used on the battlefield, just a bit of sedation and a calm, unhurried atmosphere. The boringly thorough, monotonous queries regarding her breakfast food and Latin facilitated the half-remembered thoughts and feelings to emerge. The primary gain of repressing forbidden sexual ideas could then be relinquished in a permissive setting.

In another case some years ago, a neurologist colleague referred a thirty-three-year-old man who had weakness in both hands for one month. A thorough neurologic examination was negative. The patient was an Orthodox Hasidic Jew, and the weakness was particularly difficult for him because he was a dentist. The following account emerged throughout his three-month psychodynamic psychotherapy.

Dr. F. was born and raised in one of the Hasidic enclaves in Brooklyn, New York. His father died when he was a year old and he was raised by an overprotective, overinvolved mother who herself had stress-related asthma. She put him through college and dental school, and when he opened his office in Manhattan, she hand picked the "old witch" who was his first dental assistant. He continued to live at home and at dinner his mother would hector him about "getting married" and "producing a grandson." When this assistant left, he hired his own replacement, an attractive Jewish woman in her midtwenties but elected not to tell his mother of this decision.

The inevitable happened: He fell in love, plighted his troth, and brought her home for a Friday night introduction. His mother had an acute asthma attack requiring oxygen halfway through the brisket.

By the next morning, the patient had developed a glove-distributed weakness in both forearms and hands. He was forced to take an open-ended leave from his dental practice and put his marriage plans on hold.

He began the therapy narrating the above history and offered a view of his current conflict: to move to Manhattan, marry his fiancée, and run the risk of killing his mother in the process; or to give up his loved one and suffer the slow death of an empty life. He did not feel his paretic hands were related to this conflict but were rather an independent curse. Although not clinically depressed, he was guilt ridden and redoubled his religious observances and practices. Other ways of framing his conflict, such as autonomy and adult sexuality versus childishness and dependency, fell on deaf ears. How could he support a wife if he were virtually paralyzed? His twice-a-week sessions were devoid of dreams, fantasies, speculation, or imagination. Therapy with Dr. F. was going nowhere, when, deus ex machina, his financée had the wisdom to suggest that, after the wedding, *she* would move in with the patient and his mother. This solution immediately relieved his mother's apprehensions about separation, loneliness, and losing her son. It thereby relieved his guilt regarding his mother. In the session that he told me of this turn of events, he was visibly calmer. On his own, he enrolled in an intensive physical therapy regimen and ended our treatment two weeks later, with his hands greatly improved. So much for insight.

What are we to make of Doctor F.? He had strong motivation to get well and marry, as evidenced by his hiring his future wife, but his attachment to his mother was equally strong. His culture and his identification with it reinforced the commandment "Honor thy father and thy mother." Judith Rapoport described the treatment of a patient, Daniel, where a rabbi provided important help for this young obsessive-compulsive patient. Daniel visited him and two other rabbis who sat as a religious court and annulled vows he erroneously made to God. The results of this authoritative visit greatly facilitated the treatment.[5] I did not have the benefit of Rapoport's creative and flexible example nor of her knowledge and skill, but was focused, perhaps too much, on Dr. F.'s conversion symptom.

I'm not sure Dr. F. really understood the nature of his conflict and its relation to his weakened hands. Personality and cultural issues remained paramount in the treatment, and even though I spent a longer time with him than with Ms. E., we never entered the intrapsychic realm.

## Personality

John Oldham and Lois Morris would probably label Ms. E. as having a "dramatic personality style."[6] I would say she was a bit seductive, highly suggestible, and enjoyed being the center of attention. Compared to Dr. F., she was more in touch with her emotional life. The intense five-hour session produced an abreaction similar to a battlefield amobarbital interview with dramatic improvements.

On the other hand, Dr. F., an individual that Oldham and Morris would have described as having a "conscientious personality style," due to the same stressor that produced the conversion reaction, was exhibiting characteristics of obsessive-compulsive personality by the time I saw him. As DSM-IV characterizes it, he was "over-conscientious, scrupulous and inflexible about matters of morality, ethics or values" and showed "rigidity and stubbornness."[7]

Individuals like Ms. E. with dramatizing personalities will seek appreciation of their worth and attractiveness, especially when they become ill. They are suggestible and will respond to the prescribed medical program.

Sickness threatened Dr. F. with the danger of loss of control. He tried to cope with this danger by redoubled efforts to be responsible but his obstinacy and inflexibility only increased.

## Culture

A good description of the Catholic and mystical overlying the erotic elements of Hispanic culture comes from the pen of the Nobel prize-winning author Gabriel Garcia Márquez. In *Of Love and Other Demons* we read of a sheltered South American girl of twelve living in the Colonial era. On her twelfth birthday, Sierva Maria is bitten on the ankle by a mad dog. She develops the "symptoms" of chronic pain and mutism long after the wound is healed. Believed to be possessed, she is brought to a convent for treatment. Much of the book deals with her exorcism by the young Father Cayetano Delaura who tends to this now-emaciated girl with prayer, holy water, and sacramental oils. She entraps him into love and the outcome ends tragically. Put in psychiatric terminology, Sierva Maria manifested the conflicts of Ms. E. At the cusp of womanhood she was repressed and frightened, yet unconsciously alluring enough to influence her inexperienced and clerical "therapist."[8]

Lis Harris, a staff writer at *The New Yorker*, has written a complete and loving discussion of Hasidic Judaism in *Holy Days*. Harris described Hasidism as a "revivalist-pietistic movement" of ultra-Orthodox Judaism "that began in Poland in the first half of the eighteenth century." She goes on: "Most Hasidim are suspicious of outsiders, distrustful of the printed word, and tired of being depicted as cute but anachronistic."[9]

Marital sexuality is encouraged in Hasidism and the Commandment "Be fruitful and multiply" precedes the more familiar Ten which include "Honor thy father and thy mother." Dr. F. chose the latter to obey, and it was neurosis not religion which determined his choice. To quote Harris again, "Contrary to popular belief, Hasidim are not discouraged from enjoying sex and have as part of their inheritance a wide variety of quite explicit Talmudic and post-Talmudic exhortations to enjoy the act of love."

Judith Rapoport devotes a chapter of her splendid book *The Boy Who Couldn't Stop Washing* to the religious perspective and focuses on the phenomenon of scrupulosity. Theologic writers considered scrupulosity to be a *judicium conscientiae erroniae*—an error in practical conscience. She quotes the theologian Jeremy Taylor from 1660: "They repent when they have not sinn'd. Scruple is a trouble when the trouble is over and a doubt and when doubts are resolved."[10]

Lynn Payer, in "Borderline Cases: How Medical Practice Reflects National Culture," vividly discusses four examples of accepted medical practice, in Germany, France, Britain and America.[11]

West German medicine is best characterized by a preoccupation with the heart. For example, looking at similar EKGs, 40 percent of German physicians found them abnormal while only 5 percent of American physicians did. "The obsession with the heart—and the widespread prescription of cardiac glycosides—makes the restrained use of antibiotics by West German physicians all the more striking."

Disease in France is regarded as a disorder of the *terrain,* or constitution, a failure of internal defenses rather than an invasion from without. Much of French medicine is an attempt to shore up the *terrain* with tonics, vitamins, and spa treatments; the liver is the organ of greatest significance.

English physicians are known for their medical parsimony. They prescribe half as many drugs as their French or German counterparts and perform routine surgery half as often as the Americans. This stiff upper lip attitude of English medicine preceded the economic considerations of National Health.

"American medicine can be summed up in one word: aggressive." The number of hysterectomies and caesarian sections is more than twice as high as European countries. Disease is always caused by a foreign invader of some sort. "As one French physician put it, 'the only thing Americans fear are germs and communists.'"

## Good Psychotherapy Must Consider
## a Patient's Cultural Heritage

Most important, I think, in any treatment program is the development of a solution to the conflict so that the symptom is no longer necessary. Ms. E. will go to the next month's dance but behave in a way compatible with her conscious values and upbringing. Dr. F's solution required an intervention by his fiancée to end the conflict he faced, choosing between her and his mother: she compromised and offered to move in with him and his mother.

Conversion disorder may be more common than one thinks. When I was in the medical corps, assigned to the Fifth Infantry Division, I saw five such patients in my two-year tour of duty. All were seen by me in an emergency room setting. All were male Caucasians under the age of twenty-five who came from rural backgrounds; some had come down from the hills for the first time in their lives when they enlisted.

I have often wondered why turn-of-the-century Vienna, where Freud first described his famous cases, was so rampant with individuals suffering from conversion disorder. It is a relatively rare diagnostic entity today. Now we are confronted with near epidemics of coronary artery disease, hypertension, and asthma. I have had many patients who come to me overstressed and overcommitted, whose chief complaint is: "I have a Type A personality."

Quite beyond differences in diet and lifestyle, there have been major changes in our culture in the last hundred years regardless of whether one lives in Germany, France, Britain, or America. A century ago, the dominant influence was the repressive nature of the Victorian era. People did not talk freely about sexual matters and were expected not to think about them either. This may not have been the case in every household, but most upper-class citizens were sheltered from these matters. Conversion disorder, based on repressed wishes and memories, could flourish in such an environment.

These days we are bombarded with depictions of the most graphic sexual and aggressive behaviors on television, in the movies, and in the print media. Also, most people from all social classes have some basic psychologic knowledge, and the lingo of psychoanalysis has entered the everyday lexicon. In an era of letting it all hang out, conversion reactions can no longer "work" as a vehicle to express a major psychologic conflict.

Yet even today in modern America, there are exceptions, such as the young moonshiners I saw in the army who did not own a television or read a newspaper. Ms. E., born in Puerto Rico, whose early training was in a religious school, was raised by a family determined to shelter her from the temptations of the world. Dr. F. was raised in a Hasidic community in Brooklyn, where its residents purposely eschew everyday activities to better concentrate on the eternal truths laid down by scholars centuries ago.

We should ever be mindful of the differences in the cultural origins of our patients, as well as their character structure. We should listen to them with respect and never from a position of superiority or with a mission to undermine their heritage. It's none of our business, and it won't work.

Some years ago, I was treating a forty-five-year-old married woman who was a brilliant professor of theology at a nearby Catholic college. She was trying to work up the courage to get rid of, and ultimately divorce, an abusive, philandering husband. I saw her twice a week, on Monday and Friday. Every Friday she would decide to leave this man, but over the weekend he would beg her forgiveness, saying he had ended his errant ways. So when I would see her for the Monday session, her resolve had weakened and she had welcomed him back. After two years of treatment she was stuck. But one Friday after she left my office, she impulsively decided to take a stroll in nearby Central Park. There, unnoticed, she saw her husband arm in arm with his latest. That did it. That evening she told him the relationship was over and stuck by her guns.

"He worked on Wall Street and would never be in Central Park and 96th Street at 2:00 P.M.," she told me at our session the Monday after.

"How do you explain the amazing coincidence that both of you were unexpectedly in Central Park at the same time?", I asked.

"Oh no, Dr. Druss, it wasn't a coincidence. It was the gift of grace."

I thought for a while and said, "That's as good an explanation as I might come up with."

# FIVE

# Body Image

## *In the Eye of the Beholder*

Shortly after completing my analytic training, I began seeing a twenty-nine-year-old woman who was an assistant professor of film at a nearby college. She had been married five years to a cinematographer whom she met at work. They shared many other interests, including backpacking, fishing, and rock climbing, and couldn't wait until they could afford to leave New York City. An only child, she planned to have "at least four" herself. She came to see me because of misgivings she had about combining a demanding career with her hope to devote full time attention to these future children.

Mrs. D. was born in Scotland and she still spoke with a charming burr. She had been a very anxious baby and toddler and a shy little girl who clung to her mother's skirts. She had a few good friends at school but never liked group activities or team sports. The family was stern Presbyterian; she did not tell her parents that she was supplementing her meager teacher's pay by modeling furs one day per week. She was almost six-feet tall, quite elegant, and earned as much modeling one day as she did teaching the rest of the week. I met Robert, her husband, many times when he would pick Mrs. D. up after our sessions and drive her home in his vintage VW Beetle; he was an altogether pleasant man.

Four months into treatment, she told me excitedly that she was pregnant. She and Robert immediately began soliciting friends for baby apparel, frequenting thrift shops, and exhibiting other forms of nesting behavior. She had no nausea, vomiting, and little fatigue. She remained in a joyful state until the middle of the second trimester when the baby started "to show."

At this point, she complained of feeling anxious. As each week passed, her anxiety increased; she was having difficulty sleeping and concentrating. I asked her what ideas accompanied her feelings of anxiety, and she replied only that she was getting fatter and fatter without control or limit. I was not willing to prescribe anti-anxiety medication because she was pregnant, but I did try to find the psychologic cause of what was slowly becoming panic and disorganization. Was she afraid of motherhood and its responsibilities? Of course not. Was she afraid of the pain or trauma of the delivery itself or the anesthesia? Not a bit. She was becoming irritated with me. Why didn't I understand? As she kept saying, she was horrified at getting bigger. She reported a dream: She was the Hindenberg zeppelin, getting larger and larger, and as in the news clip, it exploded in flames. She confessed that she harbored continuous feelings of being physically unattractive, and this was being aggravated by the pregnancy. Now did I understand? I didn't. She was still being paid large sums for her attractiveness as a model by the furrier employer. It was confirmed daily by her husband's behavior to her and undoubtedly by the glances in the street of any man with a pulse. I was becoming quite concerned about her welfare and the future of the pregnancy. Finally, she brought me her family photograph album from Glasgow, and we looked at it together. The early pictures were of a cute, lively child. But then, as she reached her teenage years, she had gained considerable weight. She was at her present height and all her features, which looked athletic and leggy now, looked hulking and to use her words "like the starting center on the

Green Bay Packers" in the pictures of her as a teenager. Equally striking were her outfits, which seemed almost chosen to accentuate her height and girth. "This is what I'm afraid of becoming," she cried, pointing her finger and averting her gaze. She slammed the album closed and shouted that her mother had bought all her clothes, and if they were unflattering, it was by design not ignorance. "Was your mother threatened by your emerging womanhood?" "I never thought of that. I really didn't begin to slim down until I left for college and the States."

This insight offered her some temporary relief from her anxiety, but when she approached term, it returned in full force. A week before her due date, her husband called to report his own deepening concern and asked me if I could be at the hospital when she delivered. I told him I would have to think about it; such a visit seemed too personal. Mrs. D., now desperate, also pleaded that I visit her, and I promised that I would.

The call from Robert came to my answering service late one night: she had just delivered a full-term healthy girl. Could I come by the next morning? Not knowing what to expect I did, and Robert ushered me into her hospital room. There she was, lying in bed patting her now flattened belly, and on her face was a smile that I could only call triumphant. She said the delivery went without a hitch and she and her daughter were both fine. I mumbled congratulations and arranged our next appointment three weeks hence.

She resumed treatment. Her anxiety had faded and her mood was tranquil. She took to motherhood like an old hand. On two occasions when her babysitter couldn't cover for her, she brought her little girl to the session and was adept at holding her and comforting her. She was a willing partner in exploring the origins of her rivalry with her mother at puberty. Now that the crisis was over, we could pursue this major theme with leisure and it occupied the bulk of our work.

Her baby's development also triggered thoughts of her own earliest years as an infant. Things had not been as rosy at home as she had remembered initially, and there had been problems with the way her mother treated her. Unfortunately, just as we began this new exploration, her husband received an offer on the West Coast and the three of them went their way. A note from her the next year detailed the birth of a second child, a son, without repetition of a similar crisis.

## Following the Patient's Lead

On reflection, I'm not at all pleased with my handling of this case. I was filled with personal as well as pedagogic inhibitions. It was only apparent to me later that she was suffering from a body image distortion, the fear of growing bigger and bigger, rather than a reluctance to become a mother. It was hard to tune in to her chronic and then acute feelings of unattractiveness, when she seemed so robust and attractive. It was only after she insisted I see the photograph album that I could know what she was afraid of. One is hopefully a fool but once, and I have often used patients' associations and feelings about childhood photographs to great advantage since this lesson.

The diffidence about visiting her in the hospital came from me. She and her husband were not a bit uncomfortable with me entering their crèche; I was. The prohibition was reinforced by the internalized voice of psychoanalytic supervisors against just such "enactments." As her confinement approached, I had become quite concerned about her welfare, and I think this concern did get across to her. The working alliance was strong, and she forgave my beginner's lapses.

With the crisis state removed after her delivery, she began to explore the rivalrous relationship with her mother. Both her parents were anhedonic and anti-hedonic, and both took offense at her expressive and exhibitionistic behavior as an adolescent. She felt her mother was content with a cute but anxious child but was competitive with the arrival of a developing teenager in the family triangle. The patient, who had been socially phobic, wished to maintain her dependent status on this mother. So they both participated in a collusion: she would become fatter and fatter. Her father had been an accomplished athlete in Scotland and no doubt welcomed a child companion in his games; he too was more comfortable with a fellow jock than he was with a model.

Mrs. D. and I were unable to understand the origin of the quasidelusional intensity of her body image distortion in late pregnancy. Intellectually she knew that she would be returned to her former state at delivery, but emotionally she was in the thrall of powerful forces that must have originated in earliest childhood.

The classic psychoanalytic view described by Carol Nadelson looks at how a girl's oedipal rival, her mother, is also her source of dependency gratification. Using this psychoanalytic paradigm, the successful achievement of motherhood may be seen by some patients as aggressive acts against their own mothers.[1]

Dinora Pines also suggests that if a little girl has not been successfully mothered in the earliest years of life, she will never make up for this basic loss of well-being in her body image. A woman, pregnant for the first time, will experience a normal regression. For those women with inadequate mothering in their earliest years, primitive anxieties and conflicts may be reactivated.[2]

Daniel Stern, the great genius of observing mother-infant interactions, discusses the psychotherapy technique of new mothers in *The Motherhood Constellation*. It requires the therapist to establish a different therapeutic alliance from that usually sought. Stern feels that it is often the new mother who senses they have moved outside the influence of the traditional oedipus complex motif and entered a different psychic zone that has escaped psychiatry's official theories. The therapist must follow the patient's lead when treating a new mother. The therapist should become more active, less abstinent, freer to give direct advice, and make hospital or home visits. He or she should be more focused on assets and strengths and less on pathology and conflicts.[3]

I have seen successful career women after a three-month maternity leave suffer from agony each morning when they have to part from their newborn. It is often the healthiest women who suffer the most. They enter a state of beatific revery when they describe the appearance of their little one to me. I have found that this postpartum interlude can be therapeutically unique. She is able to see her own parents' behavior to her child from a new vantage point: Were my mother and father this way to me? Memories of her childhood, especially the birth of younger siblings, come crashing down on her, and she is able to report them vividly to the therapist.

Much of this is speculative as far as Mrs. D. was concerned. She had to leave treatment with her husband before any of the hypotheses about her earliest mothering could coalesce into an integrated narrative.

At approximately the same time, I was asked to see someone that the plastic surgery service was concerned about. Mr. E. had arrived at their clinic requesting silicone implants for his temples which he felt were too narrow. His litigious reputation preceded him. He was involved in frivolous lawsuits with two other New York City surgeons. Our own plastic surgeons had already decided not to operate and hoped I could help him enter psychiatric treatment. I saw Mr. E. three times at the clinic and the following is a digest of the interviews with him.

Mr. E. was in his twenties and rather handsome. He was dressed in an exaggerated Ivy League look, with well-pressed khaki pants, blue blazer, and an ascot in his open collar. His temples appeared normal. He was very irritated at seeing a psychiatrist in a surgery clinic. He felt his complaint wasn't being taken seriously, and that he was regarded as a "psycho" case. I did not contradict this opinion and sympathized with his sense of dismissal. Mr. E. had left college in his junior year, when his mother died. He was so preoccupied with his wish to get his deformity corrected that he was unable to study or work. I asked how he supported himself, and he said with a small inheritance from his mother. Mr. E. slowly became less guarded. On the next occasion, when he mentioned his narrow temples, I again didn't contradict him but asked for his own theory as to the cause. He was pleased to get a chance to plead his case at last. He had been told he was delivered by a dangerous procedure, "high forceps," and that it had permanently damaged his skull. His mother had shown him a picture taken just after birth; he had an elongated skull and it had looked grotesque. Anyway, the obstetrician was Dr. Granowski (not his real name), "a Jew, who wouldn't hesitate to use an experimental procedure on me." The plastic surgeon at Mt. Sinai Hospital was "obviously Jewish as well and deserved to be sued."

I said that I wasn't present at his birth and could make no comment, but there were a few matters of fact I might correct if he liked. Yes. First, "high forceps," refers to the baby high in the birth canal, not forceps high on the baby's head, and if it is risky, it is so for the mother and not the baby. As you know, I added, they often do caesareans instead these days. He smiled—he had already researched this point on his own. As to the "newborn snapshot," all babies look a bit grotesque at birth, long-headed, even hairy (he nodded), and it rights itself within a week. At last someone is leveling with me, he said. Would you like to talk further about this with a colleague of mine? I avoided discussions of his anti-Semitic ideas and in this small window of opportunity I gave him the name of an older Irish psychiatrist, Dr. Y. They met, worked together, and Mr. E. was able to put off his wish for plastic surgery and the need for legal compensation, although his feelings about his deformed skull were unchanged. Three months later, Dr. Y. told me that he had dropped out of treatment.

## Finding "What Is Right" in
## What Mistrusting Patients Say

When I saw this patient, I remembered the wise words of my teacher, Dr. Lawrence Kolb, about litigious, paranoid patients. "Don't be a district attorney. Don't find out what's wrong in what they say, but what is right." To have confronted this young man about the somatic delusion of his "narrow temples" would have put me in the class of all who had failed him. A delusion is based on need, not on fact. And there was some truth in what he felt. He was being regarded as a "psycho" by the surgeons. High forceps delivery was dangerous. By acknowledging these truths and listening to his story, a temporary alliance could be built to accomplish what would really help him, a shot at psychiatric treatment.

His anti-Semitic ravings, and there was much more than I describe above, were unpleasant to hear. But it would not have served our purpose to inform him that the nefarious Dr. Granowski was, in fact, a Roman Catholic. Better to keep one's goals focused: My task was to make a referral that would stick.

Looking back, Mr. E. was suffering from a delusional disorder of a somatic type where a person has the conviction that, contrary to all evidence, a certain part of the body is misshapen or ugly. The individual is easily angered and may engage in litigious behavior when he believes he has been wronged. There is a continuum, depending on the intensity of the delusion, between delusional disorder and the less severe body dysmorphic disorder.[4]

Katherine Phillips and her colleagues reviewed thirty cases of body dysmorphic disorder. Many patients were "obsessed and tormented" by their bodily preoccupation. Avoidance of social activities became common. Many patients were depressed and even suicidal and appeared to respond better to antidepressants than to antipsychotics.[5]

Roger MacKinnon and Robert Michels discuss techniques useful in establishing rapport with these distrustful patients. Empathizing with the patient's plight will often help start a long angry diatribe that allows the interviewer to engage the patient.[6] This was certainly my experience with Mr. E. Confrontation is to be avoided; every paranoid delusion contains some kernel of truth. But rather than trying to ascertain what is true and what is created, much less directly challenging the patient, we must respond to the patient's preoccupation with his symptom and how it interferes with a constructive life. Even if Mr. E. had had narrow temples as a result of obstetric mismanagement, it would be foolish for him to be spending his life trying to get restitution for it.

I don't recall any information about his parents or upbringing or whether he gave me any details. The somatic preoccupation describes a sense of being damaged from very early on, put in body language and body metaphor. The damage occurred at the hands of another. Heaven only knows what trials this poor young man suffered as a child.

Shortly thereafter, Dr. Y. asked me if I would see his father who was recovering from a stroke at the Columbia Neurologic Institute. Mr. Y. was in his late seventies, a retired policeman who was recently widowed. Dr. Y. said that his father was more surly, more grouchy, and more testy than ever and was refusing to participate in the physical therapy and rehabilitation of his left hemiparesis.

Mr. Y. looked like a mess. He was propped up in bed, unshaven, hair unkempt, his breakfast tray untouched. His left arm was in a sling, but he spoke without difficulty. In contrast to other patients I have presented here, I recall nothing of our interaction, except his angry wail toward the end of an hour's visit, "I feel so ugly." I had met Mr. Y. once before at his wife's funeral, and although sad, he had walked with dignity and proudly with his fellow policemen beside him. Now he was depressed.

Currently used safe antidepressant medications were not available, and he was not of a mood or temperament to respond to psychotherapy, at least not with me. I went to the head nurse, and collecting some IOU's, requested that he be assigned to a student nurse as a special project with the further stipulation that she be Irish.

I returned for a follow-up in two days. When I came in, Mr. Y. had his hair combed, his face shaved, and was being washed by a very pretty young lady from the old sod. "Out," he commanded. "Can't you see I'm being attended to?" Dr. Y. called them "the beauty and the beast" and said the young nurse had fussed over him, bathed him, scolded him, accompanied him to physical therapy, and put him to rights. These two microvisits were the entirety of my consultation.

The statement, "I feel so ugly" (quite beyond the reality of his defective left arm), can have at least three metaphoric meanings to patients:

- Ugly = bad. Many patients reflect their anger, guilt, or evil inclination by feeling that their body or a part of it is unattractive. It does not require a real focus like a weakened arm in a sling. Literature is filled with characters like Mr. Hyde and Richard III whose badness is depicted for all to see in their appearance.
- Ugly = unloved. Just as it is the ugly orphan who won't be adopted, or the runt of the litter who will starve, one can feel ugly when one is not cherished. The opposite is also true. Because she feels cherished and desired, Maria can sing "I feel pretty" in *West Side Story*.
- Ugly = emasculated. A common metaphor is to equate beauty with function. For men, especially, perhaps "can't do" is the same as being physically repellent.

For Mr. Y., I think it was a lot of reason two and a bit of reason three. He had not gotten over the loss of his wife and her fussing concerns. He could submit to the young Irish nurse's intimate care without embarrassment and without further loss of face. A young male psychiatrist was not acceptable.

In a biblical story, the aged King David had a chill and was unable to warm his ancient bones, nor did the ministrations of his physicians and wise men cure his chill. [Kings I,1] But they sent for a young maiden, Abishag the Shunammite, and put her to bed with the king, and he was warmed. The biblical passage continues, "and he knew her not." It was maternal, nonerotic care that healed him. One imagines the old warrior telling her about his great victories over the Philistines many years before; some young person like Abishag who would be impressed by what he had been, not by what he was.

But according to his son, Mr. Y. also had derived much of his identity from having been a cop, one of New York's Finest. He had never taken well to retirement. He must have felt, "How can I enforce the law with only one good arm?" The young nurse must have made him, like King David, feel like a man again whether with one good arm or two. Very likely, she was like the young women from Ireland when he was in the heyday of his manliness. With something like this in mind, I had requested a nurse who might be his Irish Abishag.

## Discussion

In 1923, Freud proclaimed that "the ego is first and foremost a bodily ego." The sense of self is painfully acquired by the child through perceptions and sensations, especially those arising from the skin.[7] Wilhelm Hoffer elaborated on this notion by proposing that the infant recognizes "self" because it produces sensation in the area being touched as well as the hand, while "non-self" produces only one sensation in the hand.[8] Paul Schilder, in an otherwise impenetrable book, defines the body image as "the picture of our own body which we form in our mind, that is to say the way in which [our] body appears to ourselves." He suggests that the body image is constant throughout the lifetime of an individual.[9] In 1975, Lawrence Kolb reviewed the development of the body image and includes a rich discussion of the neuropsychiatric elements such as the development of a phantom limb.[10]

Contradicting Schilder, others have demonstrated the capacity of the body image to evolve in later life after major surgery, such as ileostomy,[11] colostomy,[12] augmentation breast surgery,[13] and corrective orchiopexy.[14]

The three patients described here had one thing in common: they all believed they were unattractive. Superficially similar, they were otherwise very different, and their body image disorder arose from different sources.

Mr. E. was disturbed by a lifelong delusionary system. His primary affect was rage at the injustices he imagined done to him at birth when someone disfigured him. He and I did not develop a therapeutic bond, and my task was to facilitate creating one with a colleague.

Mr. Y. was depressed. He had lost his wife, his status as a policeman, and now his intact physical integrity by a stroke. His childhood and youth had been a happy one, and I could best serve him by providing him a surrogate who could restore his sense of vitality and wholeness.

Mrs. D. was a high-functioning woman in a sound and secure therapy. Her story demonstrates that even healthy patients can regress when confronted with an illness (or here a pregnancy) that resonates with a conflicted period earlier in life. Her predominant symptom was anxiety: she feared she would become ugly again. She had to be challenged, confronted, and pushed to remember, and she derived relief from the insights we struggled with. She also taught me that a good therapist has to observe patients visually as well as listen to them.

# SIX

# Supervision of Psychotherapy

I have found supervision to be a glorious experience. In my own training days I was blessed with wonderful teachers some of whom have become colleagues and friends. And now I can't imagine more enjoyment than working with bright, receptive, at times skeptical, young minds in a shared search for understanding. This process for me is a personal as well as pedagogic endeavor.

The number of people one can see in a lifetime of psychotherapy practice is perforce limited. But via the words and impressions of able supervisees, the number of patient contacts is greatly multiplied. This ripple effect adds to my satisfaction.

I will present two patients seen by me only through the eyes of two very different students.

I was supervising Philip, a gifted, natural-born therapist, on his first "control" case at our analytic institute. A control case is one of three or more supervised patients whose analyses are credited to a candidate's graduation. The case was going beautifully, and one day Phil asked me if he could discuss a new patient from his private practice whom he had seen for just six visits.

The woman, Mrs. J., was forty, married, and the mother of two preteen children. She had been referred by her internist when a thorough medical workup did not reveal the cause of her frequent dizzy spells, palpitations, and one episode of fainting in a supermarket. Philip had asked her for elaborations on these symptoms, also to no diagnostic avail. But he did notice one interesting thing: there was a woman in the waiting room silently knitting each time he came out to greet Mrs. J. He assumed that this was a patient of one of his two office mates with whom he shared a common waiting room. One semiholiday when his colleagues were away he found Mme. DeFarge still there knitting. He asked Mrs. J. about this and was told, "That's my friend who accompanies me here." Really? "Yes, she goes places with me," said Mrs. J. matter-of-factly.

"I'll supervise you with this woman," I told Phil. "Find out what 'goes places' means, after all she lives only a twenty-block direct bus ride from your office!"

Phil investigated. "Goes places" meant anywhere outside of the one city block she lived on! Mrs. J. would not cross the street alone. Her block contained a supermarket, a laundry, a bank, and a stationery-newspaper store. "How do you go to your kids' school?" Her husband drove her. He, it turned out, was a wealthy corporate lawyer who drove or taxied her everywhere, and her friend accompanied her when he was at work. He paid the bills, hired the help, and disciplined the children. "The family constellation is such that this phobia has been ego-syntonic. Most of her needs are conveniently met on the block she lives on," I exclaimed. "Let's get a full and extensive life history from this fascinating woman. She could be from Vienna, circa 1901."

Mrs. J. was bright and soft spoken. She was the youngest of five children and the only girl. Her parents were Polish Jews who had emigrated to New York with a small grubstake. They invested it in a mom-and-pop paint store in lower Manhattan. Both parents worked long hours. The father took on house painting assignments on weekends to keep them in the black. Almost as soon as the boys could walk, they too worked in the family paint store. The business expanded and prospered, selling wallpaper, tile, bathroom fixtures, and small electrical appliances.

The patient remembered little about her mother except that she was busy and always working. But her father was larger than life. She had two vivid memories of him. One was in midwinter; he was dressed only in his wool sweater, unloading a delivery of paint. So robust was he that she never recalled him wearing a coat, hat, scarf, or gloves. She, in contrast, always had such cold hands that he or a brother would have to tie her shoes. The setting of her second memory was their family's annual two-week vacation in the Pocono mountains where the whole family rented a bunga-low. One morning, with father at the lead, the family group was taking their postprandial constitutional when they came upon a horrible scene. A man, unconscious with pain, had stepped into an animal trap and no one could pry it from his mangled leg. With legendary strength, her father pushed the other men aside and grabbed the ends of the trap. He strained, groaned, reddened, and slowly pulled the trap apart so the others could release the victim.

Throughout her childhood, Mrs. J. was the designated baby of the family and was treated that way. She married a wealthy older widower upon high school graduation and without skipping a beat went from the care of her father directly to the care of her husband.

"Do you think this would be someone that I could con-vert to analysis?" Philip asked. "Perfect," I said. "You have your Anna O." She appeared to be suggestible and would take the word of her young doctor as enough authority to begin a full analysis. I also pointed out the phallic adoration in the second memory she had of her father and told Philip that the emergence of her sexual history in the home of four older brothers and an idealized father would be interesting to observe.

I asked Phil what he thought caused this woman to become symptomatic after so many phobic years. He said he guessed it was the sophistication of her growing children, now wondering aloud about her childlike travel limitations. "My guess too," I said.

Philip was pleased to see just how well Mrs. J. took to analysis. Her naivete proved to be a virtue, and the material cascaded forth in all its innocence. Never having read a book on psychology, she was a psychotherapeutic virgin. Her dreams in particular were fresh and undisguised.

Dream. I went to see a hairdresser. He changed my hairdo from that of a little girl to a grownup style.

Dream. I was sitting on the toilet trying to move my bowels. Nothing came out. Then all the b.m. came out of my mouth. It was disgusting.

Rather than ask for her associations to these first two dreams, Philip explained their meaning simply and directly. The first was a wish for what the analyst would provide her. The second showed realization that she must say everything, even those things which may be "disgusting." After this brief piece of introductory pedagogy, the patient was able to work beautifully with dreams.

As she became more insightful, she was less satisfied with her phobic symptoms and childish ways. She quickly dispensed with her companion and began to take taxicabs alone to Philip's office. Borrowing a hint from Freud, some gentle exhortation was used from time to time to urge her to press forth behaviorally.[1] Eventually, she crossed the street alone. Then she took the bus alone. When treatment ended, although she was still unwilling to use the subway, her horizons had greatly expanded. She felt empowered. Her husband rejoiced in her independence, and her two children, now in their early teens, sighed with relief.

Philip did a wonderful job with this patient. He was flexible, moving from a pharmacologic-supportive stance seamlessly to a psychoanalysis. Once he diagnosed her with phobia, he focused on helping her eradicate it. She was a frightened, naive woman, and Philip realized he could not just thrust her on the couch and say nothing. His few sessions of explanation created a working alliance that bore fruit throughout the four-year analysis.

As for me, I would not have encountered this fascinating patient if it were not for the privilege of supervision.

The early 1970s were the first blush of the community psychiatry movement where chronic mental patients were discharged from large state and federal hospitals and sent to local clinics for outpatient care. I was to begin a year's supervision of Walter, a senior resident at the Columbia program. "I don't have a single psychotherapy patient that would be suitable for you," he began, with a hint of irritation in his voice, "just a lot of very crazy, chronically ill people needing custodial care."

"Why don't you pick the most difficult?" I suggested, "and let's see what we can do."

He began: Mr. V. was a single, forty-three-year-old Italian-American man who had spent more than half of his adult life in Veterans Hospitals. He was unmarried, with no personal attachments, except for an older sister who cared for him when he was out of the hospital. He had never worked. Each month, when he received his army disability benefits, he would cash the check and spend it all on alcohol; when he drank, he would become psychotic and violent, get himself arrested, and more than not end up back in the VA. Walter then added, "His functional IQ is 65, so there isn't a hell of a lot to talk about."

"Walter," I said. "He came from a Veterans Hospital. Why don't you find out about his military service. Most veterans like to talk about their military service."

At our session a week later, Walter said, "I did what you suggested and it was interesting. Mr. V. had been part of the army of occupation in Europe just after World War II. He was assigned to a small town in Italy where he distributed food to the townspeople. He was proud of the fact that he would haul large kegs of reconstituted milk and ladle it out to hungry young children. He knows a bit of Italian. The kids got to know him and called him 'the milkman.'"

"Good work," I said. "Why don't we set a goal for the year of getting this man a job? It will organize his life and give him the same kind of pride he had in the army. You will need the cooperation of his sister and lots of help from Mrs. Briggs, the social worker on the service. Maybe something with children."

After lots of calls by Mrs. Briggs and lots of preparatory support from Walter, Mr. V. was given a job as a janitor in upper Manhattan. It was a religious school for children aged six to thirteen run by Rabbi Codfish (his real name!). In supervision, Walter would tell me that Mr. V. was a hard and faithful worker and that the kids loved him. Their weekly sessions dealt largely with his feelings about the work which began to change from apprehension to pride.

Walter and I then discussed what to do about Mr. V.'s paycheck. I told Walter that he and Rabbi Codfish should work out a system where the biweekly payment would be by check and not by cash, lest Mr. V. be tempted to spend it on alcohol. He was living at his sister's and had no need to carry more money than carfare.

"But he will still try to cash the check," Walter declared.

I suddenly had an idea, "Why don't you open a savings account with Mr. V. at the Chemical Bank on Broadway and 168th Street? You could spend part of every other session walking to the bank and depositing the check."

Walter, now quite intrigued, leapt at the idea. Mr. V. kept his new passbook in his breast pocket and displayed it to the world as he would an army medal.

Walter described their first session in January to me. They had gone to the bank as usual, and in addition to the paycheck entry, there was an additional entry for the $39.50 of accrued interest. On the way back, Mr. V. asked Walter about this extra money that he had not worked for. He was amazed when Walter explained that Chemical Bank was paying Mr. V. for the use of his money.

"Walter, you have turned this man into a capitalist."

Once, on a minor Jewish holiday, I chanced to see Walter and Mr. V. walking down 168th Street on their way to the bank. They were talking animatedly, and both were smiling.

I'm really quite pleased the way this supervision turned out. Walter was an M.D.-Ph.D. resident headed for a distinguished career in research. There was a gap of at least 100 IQ points between the two participants in the therapy. It was gratifying to see Walter turn from a disgruntled, somewhat arrogant young man to an enthusiastic collaborator. I had to lend Walter some of my own therapeutic optimism. It would have suited no one if I had joined Walter in complaining about the system. It was nice to see Walter's original opinion of Mr. V. change from someone not worthy of his therapeutic efforts or my supervisory time to his most interesting patient. At our end of the year wrap-up, Walter told me that the experience of treating Mr. V. had been the most important clinical experience for him in the residency.

My own experience in the army helped. I had already developed respect for those soldiers who carried out their duty with dignity and without complaint. Mr. V. wore a tie and fresh shirt every day at the rabbi's school. As to the IQ of 65, Walter learned that a good heart may be worth as much as a good mind.

And finally, although it was not going to work in every case, it was rewarding for both Walter and me to see that at least some chronic mental patients can rejoin society and become productive members in it.

### Worth a Thousand Words

I try to avoid discussion of theory when I supervise residents; it takes us away from the case at hand and can lead to intellectualization. However, when Evan, a PGY-IV resident, asked me about the concept "repression," I attempted to answer. I gave him a standard textbook definition, but he shook his head. I then tried to tell him about "knowing and not knowing something at the same time" with a few examples from everyday life. The lights still did not go on. Evan was a young man with a background in fine arts, and I described a cartoon that I had seen in *The New Yorker* magazine some twenty years before which still made me smile:

> The cartoon covers an entire page. We are in the Metropolitan Museum of Art and the cartoon is dominated by an enormous canvas, *The Rape of the Sabine Women*. Three Roman soldiers on horseback, each with lecherous smiles on their faces, are in the center of this florid baroque canvas. Three Rubenesque women are being abducted, and

from the gleeful smile on their faces they clearly do not mind the abduction. The whole canvas had a libidinous if not bawdy flavor to it.

Our eye then moves to the floor of the museum just in front of the painting where a woman is copying the work in oils on her very small canvas. Her back is to us, but her dowdy black dress and severe bun suggest the archetypal schoolmarm. She is intent on painting, well out of the center of action, a small bluebird in the lower right corner of the canvas.

Evan laughed, "Well, Dr. Druss, I now know what repression is and won't forget it."

The funny, sad woman in the cartoon was attracted, and unconsciously aroused, by this ribald painting with its depiction of forbidden sexuality. She sat beholding it each day as she perfected her own small canvas. But the painting horrified and frightened her as well, so that instead of transcribing the central theme, she copied the innocent bluebird at the periphery. It was this quality of "knowing and not knowing" at the heart of repression, that I tried to explain to Evan. The young teenager in chapter 4 was similarly excited by, and frightened of, the coming Friday night dance. Her solution was to have physical symptoms: paralysis and deafness.

Just like there must be different approaches to creating a working alliance with each new patient, there must be flexibility in creating a supervisory alliance with each new trainee. Walter was a brilliant scientist who needed to go his own way, free to be humanized by his encounter with the patient. Evan had trouble with concepts and needed more direct instruction. Since he had an artistic mind, it was fortuitous that I could recall a cartoon, in a museum setting, to help him understand.

## Parallel Process

The unique aspects of the supervisory relationship have been written about. In 1963, Jacob Arlow described an interesting phenomenon. A candidate who was in supervision with him was treating a young male homosexual patient. The therapist depicted the patient as acting submissive with strong men, hoping to get their power by acts of submission. In a dream, the patient saw himself lying on the couch, turning around to face the analyst, and offering him a cigarette. "At this point in the supervision," Arlow says, "the therapist reached for a pack of cigarettes, took one himself, and though he knew very well I do not smoke, extended the pack to me and asked, 'Do you want a cigarette?'" Arlow did not label this phenomenon in 1963, but in this brilliant paper he was the first to describe parallel process. He described another supervisee who was relating a session in a hypomanic manner. When he stopped for breath, Arlow came to realize that the *patient* was behaving in a transiently hypomanic manner. The therapist, making the necessary identification with the patient's defenses, was acting them out in the supervision![2]

In 1980, Helen Gediman and Fred Wolkenfeld coined the term "parallel process," a phenomenon where supervisees manifest to their supervisor many psychic patterns which parallel processes that are prominent in the interaction with their patients. The essential mechanism of parallelism is identification. The student identifies with the patient to treat him and with the supervisor to learn from him.[3]

## The Epaminondas Effect

Another phenomenon that I have regularly noticed occurs particularly with good and responsive supervisees. I call it the "Epaminondas Effect." In the Southern folktale, there was a little boy named Epaminondas. He would always be exactly one step behind his mother's suggestions. For example, one day his aunt gave him a piece of cake to bring home to his mother. Epaminondas took it in his fist and held it tight, and by the time he got home there wasn't anything left but a fistful of crumbs. His mother, reviewing this state of affairs, suggested he should put it on his head and come directly home. But on the next visit to his aunt he was given a pound of butter. Obeying his mother, Epaminondas put the pound of butter on his head and it melted in the noonday sun.[4]

For example, one may suggest to a student that they get more information about a patient's paucity of friends. This suggestion the supervisee dutifully follows in the next four sessions, meanwhile the patient has had a momentous visit from a long lost parent. An episode ignored! The supervisee sees the patient two to four times a week whereas I see the supervisee but once. Let me say again that it is only the good trainees who exhibit the Epaminondas Effect, until even they learn better.

### Supervision and Mentoring

One way I regard supervision of psychotherapy is as a form of mentoring, and the best discussion of that process is contained in *The Seasons of a Man's Life* by Daniel Levinson.[5] "The mentor fosters the young adult's development by believing in him or her, sharing the youthful dream and giving it his blessing . . . " The mentoring process can cross gender and age barriers but is ideally a half-generation apart. "Through his own virtues, achievements, and way of doing things, the mentor can be an exemplar that the protégé can admire and seek to emulate." I am impressed by how much learning in supervision occurs via identification with a supervisor, rather than by direct pedagogic instruction. The mentor-protégé relationship is a transitional one, somewhere between parent and peer and can end when the protégé achieves full status. But the supervisee internalizes the relationship and his or her personality is enriched as he makes the mentor an intrinsic part of him- or herself.

Although nominally a supervisor, I have served as an advisor, career counselor, editor, and theater and movie guide. But never as a second analyst. Some supervisors, under the guise of smoking out countertransference problems in their supervisees, cross the line and pry into their personal lives. Since the supervisee is a captive audience, he or she fears offending the supervisor who has an evaluative as well as pedagogic function. Thus, students succumb to this unpleasant boundary violation and are fearful of saying, "Thanks, but no thanks." My own three analytic supervisors never pried and referred my various countertransference bloopers to the proper forum—my own analysis. I recall that one teacher in child psychiatry gleefully leapt on the fact that I had a younger sister. I was treating an eneuretic girl of ten, and he totally ignored the patient and her treatment, asking only about me and my sister. That is the way supervisors who anoint themselves as auxiliary analysts behave. They stare with humorless facies, give little feedback, and heaven help you if they should offer a word of praise.

Finally, one needs to remind supervisees to focus on the outcome of their psychotherapy, not just the process. I have taught the introductory course in psychoanalytic technique at Columbia for almost twenty years. I often ask the new candidates in their first class, "What is the goal of psychoanalysis?" They may reply, "Making the unconscious con-

scious." (Freud, 1917)[6] Or "Where there was id let ego be."
(Freud, 1933)[7] "You have spoken well," I tell them, "but these
are components of the *methods* of psychoanalysis which you
will learn with profit—not the *goal*. The goal is to heal the
sick."

# SEVEN

# The Spiritual Life of Patients

Psychiatry and psychology have cast a jaundiced eye at religion—if they have looked at all. Surveys of the directors of psychiatric residency and psychology internship programs reveal that training in the assessment of patients' religious concerns is often lacking. This omission is particularly striking, given that 74 percent of Americans report a belief in God.[1] David Lukoff and his colleagues say that mental health professionals have indeed tended to ignore or even to pathologize the religious and spiritual dimensions of the lives of our patients.[2]

Freud in *Obsessive Acts and Religious Practices*[3] began his lifelong attack on religion by stressing the similarity between religious "ceremonials" and compulsive acts. In *Totem and Taboo*[4] Freud traduces religion by emphasizing the infantile roots of religious belief; and in *The Future of an Illusion*[5] he avers that religion derives from wishful illusions based on infantile feelings of helplessness. Men knew they had disposed of their Father by violence and in their reaction to that impious deed, they determined to respect His will forever more.

The best studies of the salutary role of religion have been in medical patients; so we will concentrate on these. In fact, a number of studies have documented that the religious beliefs of medical patients can improve their capacity to cope with their illness.

In 1992, Harold Koenig and his colleagues investigated the belief systems of 850 men aged 65 and older who were admitted to a Veterans Administration medical or neurological service. Twenty percent reported that religious thought or activity was their most important strategy in coping with their illness. Depressive symptoms in these patients were inversely related to religious coping. Patients reported that faith in God, Bible reading, and frequent prayer gave them comfort and a feeling of peace. The authors feel that a positive religious experience may be especially helpful to older or more severely disabled patients.[6]

Bradley Courtenay and his colleagues agree and feel that as one ages religion will increase in importance as a coping mechanism for serious illness. They further feel it is especially important in the oldest-old and quote a Mr. Charles C., 101 years old: "I don't worry about the future; it's in God's hands."[7]

Integral to a more humanistic educational approach is educating medical students and psychology interns so that they will be more receptive to patients when they wish to talk about those beliefs which give meaning to their lives.[8] As a matter of fact, says Jeffrey Levin in 1997, five years ago only three U.S. medical schools taught courses on religion and spiritual issues as part of their core curriculum; now there are thirty.[9]

How can we as therapists best listen to the spiritual yearnings of our patients and be of greatest help to them regardless of our own religious beliefs or lack thereof? I will present two individuals for discussion and comment, neither of whom were my patients. They were, however, spiritual men who derived great comfort and strength from their religious backgrounds and beliefs.

## Joseph Cardinal Bernardin

Joseph Bernardin was born in Columbia, South Carolina, in 1928. He was ordained a priest in 1952 and archbishop of the Archdiocese of Chicago in 1982. He was elevated to the College of Cardinals in 1983. He was chairman of the U.S. Bishops' Committee that drafted the pastoral letter on war and peace. He received the Medal of Freedom at the White House two months before he died of pancreatic cancer.

The first sign of the cancer that killed him was urine darkened by bilirubin. Bernardin then had a thorough workup including pancreatography and was told that this imaging test revealed cancer of the pancreas. We don't get his immediate emotional response in his beautiful autobiography, *The Gift of Peace,* written during the three years between diagnosis and death, but we do get his own "free associations" in book form.[10] His father died of cancer when Joseph was six.

> Ever since childhood I have known that cancer changes lives—not only the life of the person carrying it, but also the lives of friends and family members who love and care for that person. . . . Today I often think of my father because he was a brave man who handled his cancer with great dignity. . . . [At age 5] I was sitting on a metal railing on the porch of our friend's home, when suddenly I fell backwards, hit the ground, and started crying. My father immediately jumped over the rail and picked me up. As he held me in his arms, I could see blood soaking through his shirt. Today I know that he is alive in me in more ways than I had ever imagined.[11]

His associations then go to his mother. She raised Joseph and his sister Elaine. He had seen her care for his father during the latter's bout with cancer. "I believe, however, as my mother always has, that family goes beyond blood lines. . . . As I started reaching out to other cancer patients and people with illnesses, I thanked God for what my mother had taught me through her own strength and kindness."[12]

Even while in the hospital recovering from surgery, he began to visit other cancer patients. "We may feel sorry ourselves or become depressed, but by focusing on Jesus' message—that through suffering we empty ourselves and are filled with God's grace and love—we can begin to think of other people and their needs."

Cardinal Bernardin became the unofficial chaplain to cancer patients in his archdiocese personally, and through calls and letters.

Bernardin began to receive daily radiation treatments and supplementary chemotherapy starting July 10, 1995. A major side effect was osteoporosis with painful secondary fractures. Fifteen months of freedom from the cancer itself ended on August 28 when an MRI revealed recurrence, and Bernardin was told he had a year or less to live. At a news conference on August 30, he said that he had learned "to look upon death as a friend, not an enemy."

Bernardin felt that "Jesus the Good Shepherd is one who lays down his life for his people," and so he had pledged to live his remaining days as a good shepherd for his own flock.

I am aware of all the methodologic pitfalls of psychobiography and psychoautobiography but am emboldened to go on because the material is so important. His short book, written under the cloud of impending death, is not only an autobiography but also can be seen as a reverie. Three factors emerge.

1. *Identification with a Brave Parent.* Joseph Bernardin was raised in a close, loving family. He admired and identified with his stoical father who himself was a cancer victim. His fa-

ther exhibited no self-pity and tended to his young son until the very end. As with the cases I previously described, identification with a brave parent is an important positive factor in patients' courage when facing severe illness.[13]

2. *Altruism.* Cardinal Bernardin did not wallow in narcissistic self-pity. At the very moment of recovering from his own surgery, he began to tend to the needs of other cancer patients, as his father had done for him. This enormous capacity for caring deeply for the needs of others was a central focus of his character and became a central focus of his ministry. (It was true on an institutional level as well, where he pioneered reconciliation between Catholics and Jews, such that at his death many Jewish people mourned the loss of "our Cardinal.")

3. *Belief in a Divine Helper.* Cancer patients have many fears as the disease progresses: pain, disfigurement, helplessness, and loss of control. But the fear of existential loneliness may be the most terrifying; it has little to do with the presence or lack of company. Its origins resonate with fears of separation in earliest childhood. An old friend, Father Henri Nouwen, spent time with Cardinal Bernardin.

> If you have fear and anxiety and you talk to a friend, then those fears and anxieties are minimized and could even disappear. People of faith who believe that death is the transition from this life to life eternal, should see *it* as a friend.

Father Nouwen was not only proclaiming a truth that was theologically meaningful to Bernardin but was at the same time being a friend by listening empathically.

The other companion that Bernardin seeks is the Lord. "We must believe that the Lord loves us, embraces us, and never abandons us especially in our most difficult moments.

This is what gives us hope in the midst of life's suffering and chaos."

The Group for Advancement of Psychiatry monograph, *Caring for People with Physical Impairment: The Journey Back*, is so named because the authors view the process of rehabilitation as an odyssey, in which a caregiver accompanies each patient along part of this metaphoric trip.[14] For Cardinal Bernardin, the trip was to eternal life where he believed that God would be his constant companion.

### Rabbi Milton Steinberg

In 1950, two years after his death at the age of 46, Rabbi Milton Steinberg was eulogized by Mrs. Ogden Reid, editor of *The New York Herald-Tribune,* "There was his brilliant mind and his eloquence, but shining through his words was his compassion and his passion for justice."[15] Eight years before his death, he suffered a near fatal heart attack in Texas but lived the remaining eight years in New York City with a full and demanding schedule. He was the author of eight books, including the beautiful novel *As a Driven Leaf* and *Basic Judaism,* a popular text used by many colleges and seminaries in their courses on Judaism.

His home was lined with books in Latin, Greek, and Hebrew, and he was fluent in all these languages. One of the outstanding theologians of his time, he was as familiar with the Neibuhrs and Tillich, with Royce, Pierce, Hartshorne, and Kierkegaard, as he was with the contemporary Jewish thinkers, Kaplan, Herberg, and Salomon. His final uncompleted project was to be a novel dealing with the love of the prophet Hosea for his wayward spouse. Arthur Cohen says:

> The novel was never finished but the closing years he lived what Hosea understood; for over and above all genius Mil-

ton Steinberg was inexplicably gentle and warm, understanding and compassionate. His books will survive the memory of his person, but those who remember his presence will not recall his writings. They will recall that this was a rare creature who so loved his Creator that he could withhold from love no man.[16]

Shortly before his death, Steinberg wrote "To Hold With Open Arms," perhaps his most famous sermon. He begins with the briefest description of the recovery from his first heart attack in Texas. "After a long illness, I was permitted to step out of doors. And, as I crossed the threshold sunlight greeted me. So long as I live I shall never forget that moment."[17] He then notices other people pursuing their everyday lives, oblivious to the wonder of the sunlight and he says, "I want to urge myself and all others to hold the world tight. For it is precious, ineffably; precious and we are careless, wantonly of it." Yet at the same time he realized that holding tight was but half the truth. "It is not only the sunlight that must slip away—our youth goes also, our years, our children, our senses, our lives. Perhaps it would have been better, he mused, to preach the doctrine of letting go, the doctrine of Goethe who said: thou shalt renounce." And Steinberg presents the paradox, "Life is a privilege—cling to it! And thou shalt renounce!" To hold one's existence dear and cheap at the same time is the paradox that captures this truth.

Finally, Steinberg says for him it is God who resolves this terrible contradiction. Given God, everything is more precious.

The sunshine in Dallas was not a chance effect. It was an effect created by a great Artist: it came from God's brush. All of life is more treasurable because a great and Holy Spirit is in it . . .

And yet, it is easier for me to let go. For these things are not, and never have been mine. They belong to the universe and the God who stands behind it. True, I have been privileged to enjoy them for an hour, but they were always a loan due to be recalled . . . and I let go of them the more easily because I know that as parts of the divine economy they will not be lost . . . the dreams of the heart, and my own being, dear to me as every man's is to him, all these I can well trust to Him who made them.

He concludes: "Only because of Him is it made possible for us to clasp the world, but with relaxed hands; to embrace it, but with open arms."[18]

I first met Jonathan Steinberg, my oldest friend, and the elder son of Milton, when I was three-and-a-half years old. We had a misspent childhood tracking Nazi spies, tormenting local shopkeepers, and making atomic bombs with our chemistry set. I must have spent at least as much time in the Steinberg household as I did in my own, or so it seemed, as viewed through the lens of idealizing youth.

With one exception it was not a sick man's household, that being Mrs. Edith Steinberg's unceremonial removal of guests, both the famous and ordinary, at the slightest sign of Milton's fatigue. Other than that it was the office-home of a lively and brilliant scholar. Students from the very young to the ancient, alone or in groups, would come for their turn to sit at his feet. Young people especially (me included) adored him. I recall that conversations with evening guests were timely and passionate.

Of course, what I most cherished were the brief but countless one-on-one encounters: watching and laughing together at a bit of staged wrestling on television; being quizzed on my Latin declensions; or being listened to with a bemused intensity and compassion that I have with others tried in vain to recapture.

So it was with special interest that I came upon the last months of Joseph Cardinal Bernardin. Although these two men hail from different theologic backgrounds, you cannot help but see many personal similarities: their kindness, gentleness, and compassion. Also, each put his illness behind him and to the consternation of loved ones devoted the end of his life to the care and instruction of others.

## Control of Pain

The cornerstone of any treatment program for the declining and deteriorating patient is proper control of pain; without this all other programs will be useless. Full discussion of this topic is beyond the scope of this slim volume and of most therapists' needs. Suffice it to say, the therapist should seek to ensure that the oncologist, anesthesiologist, nurse, or whoever has primary care for the patient is providing enough analgesic and giving it as often as needed. One notices a misplaced parsimony in dispensing narcotics: too little or too infrequent. Cleeland in a recent editorial in the *JAMA* stated that the degree of both acute cardiac pain and chronic cancer pain is regularly underestimated by caregivers.[19] We serve patients by reassuring everyone concerned that they will not become addicted, and that it would be irrelevant if they did.

I saw an interview on public television filmed in England with the great Dennis Potter, author of *The Singing Detective*. It was conducted when Potter was in terrible pain from terminal pancreatic carcinoma. Potter was brilliant, open, ironic, and witty only because he had a hip-flask filled with elixir of morphine from which he drank often. Could the reader imagine this humane and sensible approach to terminal pain approved by our state and federal legislatures?

## The Healing Power of Words

The eminent Boston cardiologist Bernard Lown in *The Lost Art of Healing* describes a patient two weeks after his heart attack, who was still in coronary intensive care with virtually every known complication.[20] He was expected to die any hour and had a "do not resuscitate" order in his chart. One morning he looked better, felt better, and all vital signs were much improved. Lown could not explain the improvement and proclaimed it a "miracle." The patient was well enough to be discharged and returned for follow-up in six months. At that time he told Lown that he had heard him tell everyone on rounds to listen to the patient's "wholesome gallop," and believed he couldn't be dying. Lown writes that the patient was unaware that a gallop was a bad sign generated by a failing left ventricle and thus a wholesome gallop would be an oxymoron. Lown concludes that even when the outlook is doubtful, optimism and affirmative words promote well-being if not always recovery.

Another patient was a woman who was sliding downhill day by day until Lown asked her what was wrong. She said one day on rounds the revered Dr. Samuel Levine had uttered the letters T.S. (tricuspid stenosis) in describing her benign murmur. She believed T.S. meant "terminal situation" and could not be convinced otherwise.

## Accompanying the Patient

At times the patient who is in the final stages of disease will need no more but no less than a listener. Relatives may be too upset and other physicians too busy, but the therapist who is most trained in listening may be the ideal companion.

Walter Benjamin writes of the healing power of hands.[21] He says that dying people suffer from "skin starvation"; it is easy to touch babies and healthy children but harder to touch "those whose bodies reveal decades of entropy and the brokenness no human science can repair." Unfortunately, therapists are poorly trained in the laying on of hands since it is rightly prohibited from the bulk of their work. They must understand that terminal patients have regressed to a stage where they experience only the most archaic transferences, where the caregiver is someone they can hold. While visiting a cardiac ICU, Benjamin saw that technology rather than a person accompanied the acutely ill in dying as they enacted their final rite of passage: "Physicians can enter the lonely world of the dying patient when they affirm the healing power of their own unique humanity."

The stoic philosophers and poets of ancient Rome believed that temperance, discipline, and self-reliance would lead to a life of serenity. Horace wrote, *"Aequam momento rebus in arduis sevare mentem*—Be sure to keep a level head in difficult times and circumstances." (Horace: Odes II, 3)

But what shall we do when our own strength fails us, when we can no longer rely on our enfeebled bodies and troubled spirits, and we must turn outside our own diminished resources? We can then say with the author of the mighty Hebrew hymn *Adon Olam*

> I place my soul within his palm
> Before I sleep, when I awake,
> And though my body I forsake
> Rest in the Lord in fearless calm.

# EIGHT

# Termination of Psychotherapy

*Patient's Goals, Therapist's Goals*

## *Patient's Goals*

Ms. M., a twenty-two-year-old single student nurse, was referred to me early in my years of practice because of anxiety symptoms which began when she arrived in New York City. She was born in Empire, a small city in upstate New York, and told me she came to Columbia for her nurse's training specifically to meet and marry an eligible young man, hopefully a doctor. Raised in a rather protective Roman Catholic family, she had found both the nursing school and the New York City setting uncomfortable, frightening, and not at all what she had expected. The exposure of bodily parts at the bedside and the freedom of behavior in New York City was frightening to her, and she said she was suffering from "culture shock." She was an attractive, intelligent young woman and was the only one in her family who had completed college. We began a psychodynamic psychotherapy twice a week with a one-and-a-half-year limit before her graduation, when she would return to Empire. Her anxiety quickly abated without medication as she began to find comfort in the treatment setting. Much of the time was spent on dating behavior and big-city mores. She said at the outset that she was not prepared to lose her virginity until her wedding night but she would like to be free to engage in other physical intimacies with young men that would be more in keeping with the cultural norm of 1970. As we discussed her parental upbringing, repressive even for small town America, she began to date and allow herself to enjoy physical closeness. Her bedside nursing improved to the point that she eventually graduated with honors. At the appointed time, the end of May, she completed her training and her therapy and returned home.

She had been especially prompt in paying her bills and when I sent my final bill to her upstate address, she paid it promptly as well, but it was shy $10. The next month I billed her for the small amount, and the following month as well, yet there was no response from her. I searched my notes for evidence of "negative transference" that might account for her failure to pay me this last bit. However, no answer was forthcoming. Then the next November, quite by surprise, I received a call from the patient saying that she would be in New York City for the holidays. Could I see her after my hours and receive her payment in person? I said "of course," and she arrived a week later at 7:00 P.M. when my last patient had departed. I buzzed her into my waiting room and went out to greet her. There she was and seated next to her was a young uncomfortable looking man with a short crew-cut who she introduced to me as Joe from Empire, New York. At this point she reached into her purse with her left hand and handed me the $10 bill dramatically, exhibiting the diamond on her ring finger.

It all became clear. She had come to me to get a husband, and the treatment was not completed until she had become engaged with plans to marry.

I learned a great deal about the *specificity of patients' goals* from this case. A man with a serious writing block did not terminate his analysis until a long overdue and promised manuscript had been accepted for publication. A woman in her early forties, who had entered treatment because of an increasingly demoralized state due to a failure to conceive, did not decide to terminate therapy until the conception occurred two years later, and she returned to present the baby in vivo three weeks after she had given birth. I have come to realize also that patients are less interested in our brilliant insights and interpretations than in the achievement of the goals they had on presentation. I have also learned to pay attention to these stated goals throughout the therapy.

Ms. N. was a fifty-one-year-old fashion designer undergoing chemotherapy for metastatic breast cancer. She came to see me with the announced goal of helping her boyfriend (of twenty years) cope with her illness and ultimate death. She said that Jonesy was "an escapee from Picasso's blue period," and she wanted a therapist "without long faces, tsks-tsks, or there-theres." I treated Ms. N. for three years; she had a wonderful sense of humor, a fierce temper, and cursed like a trouper. She had great flair and enormous energy. Except for the one event I am about to describe, she did not become overtly depressed and handled an oophorectomy, adrenalectomy, and two pathologic fractures with amazing courage.

One evening, I got a call from Jonesy that Ms. N. had locked herself in the bedroom and refused to come out. Would I come over to see her? I said, "Of course," and taxied down. When I got to her apartment, Jonesy let me in and dolefully pointed to the silent bedroom door. I knocked and said, "This is Dr. Druss. What is the matter?" No answer. "Would you please come out for a bit?" No answer. Finally, I shouted, "Damn it. I'm missing *I Love Lucy* on TV to see you and I expect some common courtesy." At last there was a stirring behind the door. After a few minutes, she came storming out and marched over to Jonesy. "What the #@% is the matter with you? Dr. Druss has come all the way down here and you haven't even served him any tea." Jonesy blew a sigh of relief and left us to our tea. "So what's the deal here?" I asked across the table. She said she had discovered jaundiced eyes and found it very upsetting. We discussed this symptom and she feared it was the repetition of an allergic response to sulfa drugs when she was twenty-one; it had led to a humiliating two months of hair loss and jaundice. Major painful surgeries more recently did not bother her half as much. At her session the next day, she was much relieved and had already decided that those #@% doctors had given her serum hepatitis from all those #@% blood transfusions (rather than the more likely possibility of liver metastases). She died quietly four months later.

Ms. N. said that she was in therapy for the long-suffering Jonesy, not herself. Her announced goal of helping another was a face-saving way of getting treatment for herself. So here we learn a second important principle. Even though a patient may say that they have come to help a lover, child, or parent, everyone enters therapy for *themselves*.

Ms. N. was making use of the defenses of healthy denial and benign displacement which are necessary in a terminally ill patient.[1] I did not shake these defense mechanisms, and it was only when the jaundice emerged as a painful repetition from the past that her salutary defenses failed her. I tried to help her resurrect her denial the moment I got to her apartment and was successful.

I first saw Mr. T. at the bedside of his wife. I had been called to see her during the course of her treatment for disseminated ovarian cancer. She and her husband were both forty-five at the time. I recall very little about the wife, except that some untoward event, most likely a stroke, ended her life a few months after my consultation. However, I did hear from Mr. T. six months later. He called me to request an appointment, saying that I was the only psychiatrist he knew. He was very demoralized regarding his wife's death and was in a state of profound grief.

Mr. T. described himself as a passive and dependent man. Although not a loner, his main source of social intercourse was through his work where he had developed superficial friends. He was a cellist in a small chamber orchestra here in New York. He was utterly devoted to his wife, the first real heterosexual attachment in his life. They had been unable to have children and there was no other family member living. He did not have any of the stigmata of a major depression but rather an empty loneliness that was all pervasive.

I saw him once a week in a supportive psychotherapy. By luck we shared many interests, especially music, and he was acquainted with most of the major musical figures and orchestras of our day. Many of the things he discussed were interpersonal problems at work, especially the ongoing conflict he had with the concertmaster of the orchestra, who was a constant irritation to the patient. We were unable to unearth much psychogenic material, except that his mother had a severe postpartum depression after his birth and declined to have any other children. Although nothing was fully resolved, at the end of a year he was feeling considerably better and we stopped the treatment.

The patient returned on and off a number of times during various disruptions in his life. One time, he came back to see me when he was diagnosed with colon polyps, discovered during a routine colonoscopy. One of these was malignant and the whole issue of cancer returned to him and revived his mourning for his wife. Other than a polypectomy, no intestinal surgery was needed. He returned another time after a brief affair with a neighbor woman that was ended abruptly by her. At this point he was depressed, and I elected to place him on an antidepressant which raised his mood from depression to his chronic state of everyday loneliness. His final visits, fifteen years after our first meeting, occurred due to conflicts over a possible move and promotion to the first cello seat of an orchestra outside of New York City. He asked for a psychiatric referral in that city. I arranged this for him, and to the best of my knowledge, he is still seeing this psychiatrist.

The case of Mr. T. illustrates yet another important point about patients' goals: They may not be enunciated at the start of therapy at all. Therapy patients may need the support of treatment on and off throughout their lives. Mr. T. needed periodic care as life stresses ebbed and flowed, and the goal varied depending on the nature of that stress. Some patients have neither the motivation nor the capacity to make a total overhaul in their psychic structure.

But perhaps I made an error here with Mr. T. Looking back I wonder whether group therapy might have been a valuable addition to his therapeutic regimen. Treatment in a group setting might very well have helped him connect socially to other people and supplemented individual support.

## Therapist's Goals

The therapist should have as a primary goal the healing and restoration of the patient. The means of achieving this goal is to free the patient from his or her symptoms, conflicts, and characterologic restraints, so that they can better achieve their own life goals. Any deviation from this axiom will ultimately lead to an exploitation. Any use the therapist makes of the patient for his or her *own* needs is a violation. It is the more subtle, often quite unerotic transactions between therapist and patient that I wish to discuss. We may all be guilty of some of them, and they are due to a confusion between patient's and therapist's goals.

Some therapists will seek tips on investments from their wealthy patients in finance; some will pump their celebrity patients for gossip. Therapists may demand graphic detail of their patients' sexual behavior, often augmented by enunciating the rule of "free association"; this practice may be solely for the benefit of the therapist's prurience. On the other hand, asking an obsessive patient to specify the movie he saw last weekend, or to name his new girlfriend, boss, or car model, will often lessen intellectualization and abstract thinking. Here insistence on detail is to help the patient, not gratify the therapist.

Therapists may be unwilling to respond to patients or can be continually silent as a way to help the patient begin a difficult search into his or her own resources. Or it can be a controlling or even sadistic stonewalling of a needy person in distress. In the same way, patients can be needlessly humiliated under the umbrella of "the truth above all." (This is not unlike "truth dumping" in general medicine where the physician can feel self-congratulatory for always "saying it straight.") The psychotherapy patient much like the medical patient is regressed and vulnerable.

Another very tricky set of transactions that occur, as therapy progresses, is the imposition of the therapist's values and lifestyle on the patient. My guess is that this situation is ubiquitous and almost unavoidable. Issues such as pace of life, attitudes to the balance of work and family, ethnocultural and religious practices are all too easily turned into prescriptions for mental health, subtly written for patients in every session.

The most formative example of this interaction in my professional development was revealed to me before I became a psychiatrist, when I was a medical intern in Boston.

The patient was a sixty-five-year-old widowed Irish Catholic woman with mild congestive failure secondary to mitral stenosis. She was pleasant and reverentially polite. I saw her each Wednesday afternoon in my medical clinic. The entire visit took fifteen minutes and included examination of her heart and lungs, her ankles, and writing her a prescription for digitalis leaf which she had been taking regularly without ill effect for ten years. Her condition had been stable for the past ten years and, our verbal encounter was a hurried review of her cardiovascular symptoms and possible side effects.

One Wednesday morning at 10:00 A.M. there was a cardiac arrest at the clinic. I rushed over with the team to help revive the afflicted man. During this process I happened to notice Mrs. O'B. already seated, talking to another patient; her appointment with me was not scheduled until 2:00 P.M. That afternoon, after our usual brief encounter, I told Mrs. O'B., "I saw you this morning at 10:00 A.M., and I hate for you to wait four hours for a fifteen-minute appointment each week. Things have really been very stable for years. Perhaps you would like to come here every other week and see how it goes." I don't recall her answer but vividly recall her appearance the next week when she was wheeled into intensive care gasping for breath, in acute pulmonary edema.

I foolishly thought I was doing this woman a favor. With my incredibly busy intern's schedule, every minute counted. In her lonely life, the four hours at the clinic were a highlight, talking to fellow patients and receptionists, seeing a doctor, and being paid attention to. At the time I realized none of this and made myself the measure of her needs.

There has been no greater mischief in the world than the misapplication of the Golden Rule, "Do unto others as you would have them do unto you." It has no place in good psychotherapy. It should be replaced by the Empathic Rule, "Do unto others as they really need to be done unto."

Another very different patient, in very different circumstances comes to mind. I received a call sometime ago from a couple who wished me to see their twenty-year-old son. He was set on giving up his premedical program to pursue playing the oboe. They wanted an opinion of his "sanity" regarding this decision, and then treatment to help him "come to his senses." I told them to have their son call me and I would get back to them after my consultation.

W. arrived and began by telling me of the seriousness of his calling. He started his love of woodwinds at six when given an ocarina for his birthday. He soon graduated to the recorder and then to the oboe. By twelve he had been playing in the school orchestra and taking private oboe lessons. He had won a number of oboe competitions and had been called a rising star by oboist Heinz Holliger.

He was a well-rounded student who had achieved a B+ average as a biology major. But, he said, he had done all this to please his parents and that his life's passion was the oboe. He had a realistic picture of his likely future, "I will be playing the oboe somewhere in Montana and earning my keep teaching oboe to disinterested schoolboys. My wife and I will lead a life of happy poverty, eating mashed potato sandwiches." He dated regularly and was currently living with a young woman, herself a musician, who had also taken vows of poverty. He asked me to intercede with his parents. After the three-visit consultation, I called his parents. "I have some bad news for you," I told them, "your son is quite sane."

Although his parents made the "referral," once W. entered my office *he* was the patient. To me, sanity was never an issue; it was his judgment. I did want to evaluate three things: (1) his dedication to the instrument, (2) his abilities as objectively judged by the music community, and (3) the reality of his appraisal of his future should he realize his plans. He came through these tests with flying colors, and since W. was my patient, I acted on *his* behalf. If this were a three-year therapy rather than a three-session consultation, I would have helped W. confront his parents and explain his dream to them. But that was not the goal.

About a year and a half later, I received a printed announcement from Salt Lake City of the birth of his son on which he had handwritten "thanks for everything."

Many level the accusation against therapists that we are the agents of the establishment, of white middle-class values. These critics further assert that to enter psychotherapy or to take psychotropic medication will endanger their creativity and expunge their individuality. Most therapists, white or African-American, male or female, are by virtue of their training people who do value a steady job and a stable home life. Also, we have personal ethics that we treasure and try to impart to our children and our students. We enter dangerous territory if we try to impose a particular lifestyle on our patients.

## Goals and Termination of Therapy

The various major modalities of psychotherapy have their own termination points.

Many highly symptomatic patients achieve the goal of symptom relief with chemical agents; the patient with biogenic psychologic symptoms can expect maximum benefit from pharmacotherapy. This is elegantly elaborated by Paul Wender and Donald Klein in *Mind, Mood and Medicine*.[2]

Interpersonal therapy with its defined number of treatment sessions boldly suggests: Let us do the best we can for our assigned fifteen or twenty sessions and be content. This fixed amount of sessions may motivate both therapist and patient.

Behavioral and cognitive therapies rely on a joint judgment in patient and therapist as to when to stop. A woman with a hand-washing compulsion may decide that a 90 percent improvement in three months is sufficient, and a flattening of the asymptotic curve of progress has been reached.

Psychodynamic psychotherapy and psychoanalysis has produced the most extensive literature on goals and termination. A wonderful example is the classic paper by Ernest Ticho, written in 1972, "Termination of Psychoanalysis: Treatment Goals, Life Goals." In it he states, "Life goals are the goals the patient would seek if he could put his potentialities to use. Treatment goals concern removal of obstacles to the discovery of what those potentials are."[3]

Ticho further says that the healthy person continues to grow while the neurotic one stands still, fixed in the past. Treatment goals include establishment of mature personal relationships, the diminution of self-centeredness, increased frustration tolerance, and a less harsh superego. He quotes Paul Schilder who wrote, "Whoever is dissatisfied with himself is always ready to revenge himself against others."

Ms. M. wanted to marry. The treatment which could have been conducted in any city focused on the liberalities of New York, the exposures in a big city hospital, and her anxious responses to them. The treatment dealt with her own inhibitions toward intimacy with men. Once improved, she was able to find Joe, a young man who was from her own backyard.

Ms. N. required two things from her therapy. First, she needed constant reinforcement of healthy defenses as she faced a terminal illness. Second, the bulk of our work together was spent unraveling the neurotic infrastructure attached to that illness. The jaundice, which might have been a minor symptom for one patient, felt catastrophic to Ms. N. because of her unique history and experience that we had discovered together. (My father sustained two heart attacks after the age of eighty with aplomb but was frightened by a foot infection. He was a pathologist who got his training before the age of antibiotics, and septicemia, his ancient enemy, meant sure death.)

Mrs. O'B. was an observant but not a spiritual person. She would tell her beads daily to the voice of Cardinal Cushing on the radio, as he intoned the rosary. She attended Mass each week. Her goal was to keep her medical condition from getting worse; she had made peace with it the way it was. Mrs. O'B. had developed an institutional transference to the hospital, as she had to the church, and any given medical resident or parish priest could change, as long as her place was secure at its bosom.

The issue of goals was more complicated with Mr. T. Patients like him may enter psychotherapy because of one problem, a "ticket of admission" as it were, and if a good working alliance has been established, they may find themselves returning time and again as other problems arise. His goals were different each time he came to see me, and a different treatment modality was required for each. At first, he needed supportive therapy for the terrible grief he felt when his wife died. Later on, antidepressants were required when he succumbed to a major depression. Group therapy would have been very helpful to complement the one-on-one dependent relationship he had made with his wife and then with me. *Flexibility*, which I have tried to stress so often in previous chapters, was maximally required with Mr. T. and for the many patients like him.

# NINE

# Patients Who Return to Psychotherapy

There are three reasons why patients return to psychotherapy. First, like Mr. T. from the previous chapter, they have never really left. Rather than undergo a proper termination they experience a series of interruptions in an ongoing process. They are always on my roster.

Second, there are patients who experience a recrudescence of symptoms due to causes that are primarily intrapsychic and internal. No one is ever completely cured, and conflicts, propensities, and inclinations remain to be revived. I have found that I had gotten to know these individuals so well that their return is usually brief and technically quite easy. Mr. H., originally discussed in chapter 2, returned, and I will discuss the episode in this chapter.

Finally, there are patients who return because external events occur that could not have been anticipated in their original therapy experience. Such events include retirement, death of a loved one, and serious illness. We will discuss Mr. Z. and how two very different therapeutic modalities for the same patient were necessary in two very different circumstances.

Mr. H., now sixty-three, returned to see me nine years after the termination of his therapy. He said that, in spite of his life going very well, he had begun to reexperience the irritability, dysthymia, and anxiety that had originally brought him to my office. These symptoms had been building up over the last month. During our first session we caught up on the nine years. He was thriving in his professorial role at a business school and never regretted selling the family business. He and his wife were, if anything, doing better financially than he had anticipated, and they had begun to travel and "see the world." His elder daughter was married, expecting a child, and his younger daughter was a star in law school. Until a month ago everything was "great."

He brought in a dream the second session. The dream was of a mathematics equation written on a school blackboard:

$$f(x) = 4 \times 4$$

This had been typical of the terse storyless dreams that Mr. H. had brought to me originally and was his signature. He began to associate and "decipher" it. It was from his days in college when he studied math and statistics to prepare himself for accounting. He had always loved mathematics and he felt such a dream must be an important encoded message from the unconscious.

"The 'f(x)' means a function of x, where 'x' was the unknown and stood for me," he began.

"Function of x" reminded him of "fuck x," which further reminded him of "father of x," and that maybe his "father was still fucking x." But how? What of the "$4 \times 4$"? Was it 16—something at age sixteen? No, it was 4. He was stuck.

Now, quite into this puzzle, I returned, "Do I recall correctly that your birthday is July 4th?" (I remembered that during his two years with me he had emphatically said that his birthdays had never been "independence days" when he was younger.) "Yes, it's June now and July 4th is coming up in a few weeks." We were on to something. "But why now?

You have been having uneventful July 4ths I presume for nine years?"

He thought for awhile and did some quick mathematical calculations. "This July 4th I will be sixty-four, the age my father was when he died. I'm outliving the old goat." He added that sixty-four was the cube of four and not the square, but he felt he had already gotten the important message of the dream.

He returned for a third and final session much relieved.

Mr. Z. was one of the first private patients I had analyzed. He was referred by his girlfriend, herself in analysis with a supervisor of mine, who suggested my name. Mr. Z. was thirty-five and single, working as a master cabinetmaker for a furniture company. His girlfriend felt he needed "loosening up."

When Mr. Z. first arrived at my office, he seemed like an unlikely customer for analysis. He spoke sparsely and carefully, with a New England twang, and was dressed in a plaid shirt and workpants. This was not an artistic pose but reflected his background; he was born in Maine to a logging family, looked and spoke like Henry Fonda in the John Ford masterpiece, *Young Mr. Lincoln*. But as I got to know him, his honesty, directness, and great intelligence emerged, and I took a great liking to him.

He described his father as an American Gothic, silent, flinty, and unforgiving. His father had opposed Mr. Z. coming to New York City, his artist girlfriend, and virtually anything deemed "impractical." Mr. Z. however, an only child, was the apple of his mother's eye and the two of them shared an interest in literature and the arts. He was an avid reader of the classics, and the only one I knew who had actually read *The Last of the Mohicans*.

He took to the couch readily but remained a man of few words. His associations were free enough but scanty. The analysis relied heavily on his vivid, often literature-inspired dreams as the royal road to *his* unconscious. He never lost his temper and rarely raised his voice. I had to adjust my ear accordingly: When he used the expletive "damn," it meant cold fury!

During the course of his four years of analysis he made two important changes in his life, and he was extremely grateful that I did not prejudge them. He "loosened up" enough to marry his girlfriend, who sounded like a lovely woman. And with his wife's support he took a huge leap of faith, left the steady employ of the furniture company and set out for himself to design his own line of wood furniture. Both these acts were taken against the strong and unforgiving admonitions of his father. Obvious oedipal issues were investigated and analyzed thoroughly. The patient had two dreams the night of his last day on the company payroll. He was Icarus flying too high and the sun melted his wings. Dedalus flying lower, at a proper height, was glowering at him. But instead of a free fall, Icarus skied down to earth averting sure catastrophe. Mr. Z. was an expert skier and felt he would "land on his feet." In the second dream *he* was Dedalus setting out in snowshoes. His association was to Stephen Dedalus at the end of *Portrait of the Artist as a Young Man* setting out with hope. But the snowshoes were handicaps. They represented his age, relative poverty, and the many difficulties in becoming a designer. He was in the midst of a positive maternal transference, sharing literature and art. The rivalry with his father was also present, and the dreams left unclear whether the brutal snows of Maine (his father) would hinder him like bulky snowshoes or could be overcome by mastery on skis.

By the time the analysis had terminated, he had established himself as an up-and-comer in American furniture design, and he was even showing a profit. The termination phase of the analysis dealt with his coming to terms with his father's disapproval and seeing himself as a success in spite of it.

Until he called me, I had not seen Mr. Z. for some fifteen years. However, during the intervening years, he sent me tearsheets from various decorating and furniture magazines that described or depicted his latest work. The two highlights, I recall, were a photograph of one of his chairs in *The New York Times Magazine* and an article in an out-of-town newspaper that called him "one of our modern American masters" when a piece of his was added to the permanent collection of the museum.

I recognized his laconic manner when he called and gasped at the bad news he had to tell me. His wife, childless, had died two years before in a terrible skiing accident. And now just recovering from that loss, he had received a diagnosis of advanced cancer of the common bile duct. This diagnosis was made by cholangiogram, and he was told that any surgery would be ineffective. Still on the phone, he told me that he had but months to live and wished to see me.

I of course agreed to see him that day. He looked much older and much thinner. But other than the occasional bouts of acute upper-right quadrant colic that had led him to seek medical attention, he was blessedly pain free. He apologized for "bothering" me but said he had no significant family, and although he had many acquaintances in the artistic world, no intimate friends.

While formerly he had used the couch, he now faced me across the desk. He looked at my old desk, its surface defaced from years of coke can and coffee cup rings, and said as he sat down, "This desk is starved for oils."

In virtually all these return sessions, he made some reference to my venerable desk. He denied depressive symptoms or even sadness and then minutes later would suggest that the spots on the desk were "the tear stains from many years of depressed patients." I stopped trying to interpret his obvious references to his own "starvation" and "depression" and allowed the desk to be a mutually understood metaphor for himself.

We had weekly sessions and he chose to speak mainly about his unfinished work and unrealized plans. I could see that he was experiencing increasing pain and discomfort as his face would scowl and contract. "Why don't you have this nice desk refinished? It shouldn't cost too much," he said one day. I decided to call someone about it and not only did they say they had to take it into the shop for two weeks to sand it down, but also quoted a rather hefty figure. I told Mr. Z. "That man is a damn mountebank," he said with more heat than anything before. "It's a one-hour job." Then he paused for a long while and asked me if he might do a "little touch up" for me the next session. I am pleased to report that I said, "I'd be grateful."

The next session, he came in with a small duffle bag. He took out some clean white rags and a perfume-sized bottle of imported linseed oil. I moved to my other chair as he applied drops of the oil with one rag and buffed with another. He was talking to me for the first five to ten minutes, but then stopped and began to whistle aimlessly as he polished the desk. The lines fell from his face and he looked totally at peace, completely engaged in the task at hand.

This was the last time I saw him. He called to say he was being admitted to the hospital for pain control three days later, and I heard from a friend of his that he had died shortly thereafter.

If someone demanded to know the most moving sessions that I have described in this book, I would reply: the one where Larry (chapter 1) spoke, and this last one, where Mr. Z. did not.

I think we can understand Mr. Z.'s wish to polish my desk in at least three ways. First, as I already stated, Mr. Z. equated the desk with himself, needing restoration. Second, Mr. Z., as his health worsened, felt the need to leave the highly cerebral world of designing furniture and return to the palpable reality of repairing it, where he had begun. He felt a special contentment in the sweetness of the wood and oil. Third, he wanted to give me a gift and repay me quite beyond the required fee for service; something to remember him by.

I made a decision long ago not to become friends with former patients, and it has served me well. I told them they can have many friends in their life but only one "me" who is available in the wings if needed. One gets to like most patients in time, and there is a special bond derived from hard work done together and a completed task well done. Many of my patients have been interesting people who have led interesting lives, but I have resisted personal invitations so as not to change the basic nature of what is primarily a professional relationship.

As far as gifts at termination are concerned, I accept them with gratitude. It may have been a book that they had written themselves or that we had discussed. It may have been a record that they had made or music that had special meaning for them. But I will not accept expensive or lavish gifts or any where the monetary value is greater than its meaning.

As one gets older, more and more patients are those who have returned for psychotherapy. For our purposes, they serve to illustrate one of the major points in this book: *the need for therapeutic flexibility and imagination*. My first treatment of Mr. Z. was a standard psychoanalysis. The second was a supportive psychotherapy; same patient different circumstances.

The need to listen to patients does not vary with the treatment modality. My ear was tinny or true in varying degrees throughout the cases presented in this book.

Just some months ago I attended a concert by the gifted young pianist Hélène Grimaud. In it she played Brahms last pieces for the piano. They were totally unfamiliar to me and sounded like a random cacophony of notes. Not willing to yield to ignorance, I bought her CD of this music and listened to it over and over again with concentration. Slowly, more and more with each new playing, the Brahms pieces took on form and meaning. I now count them as some of my favorites.

Should we do less with our patients? We must listen to the music of their words until it too has meaning, and even beauty, to us.

# Notes

CHAPTER I

1. John D. Rainer. Interpretation, communication, and understanding. *The Deaf American.* 19:43–45. 1966.

2. David Ebert and Paul Heckerling. Communication with deaf patients: knowledge, beliefs, and practices of physicians. *JAMA* 273:227–229. 1995.

3. Leah Hager Cohen. *Train Go Sorry: Inside a Deaf World.* New York: Houghton Mifflin. 1994. p. 13.

4. Oliver Sacks. *Seeing Voices: A Journey into the World of the Deaf.* Los Angeles: U. of California Press. 1989. p. xi.

5. *Children of a Lesser God.* Film based on Mark Medoff play. 1986.

6. Elizabeth Zetzel. Current concepts of transference. *Int. J. Psychoan.* 37:369–376. 1956.

7. Leo Stone. *The Psychoanalytic Situation.* New York: International Universities Press. 1961.

8. Ralph Greenson and Milton Wexler. The non-transference relationship in the psychoanalytic situation. *Int. J. Psychoan.* 50: 27–39. 1969.

9. Joseph Sandler and his associates. *The Patient and the Analyst: The Basis of the Psychoanalytic Process.* New York: International Universities Press. 1973. pp. 27–36.

10. Aaron Beck and associates. *Cognitive Therapy of Personality Disorders.* New York: The Guilford Press. 1990. pp. 64–66. and Aaron Beck and associates. *Cognitive Therapy of Depression.* New York: The Guilford Press. 1995. pp. 45–60.

11. Gerald Klerman and Myrna Weissman. "Interpersonal counseling for stress and distress in primary care settings." In Klerman, Weissman, and associates. *New Applications of Interpersonal Psychotherapy.* Washington, D.C.: American Psychiatric Press. 1993. pp. 295–318.

12. Lesten Havens. *A Safe Place: Laying the Groundwork of Psychotherapy.* Cambridge, Mass.: Harvard U. Press. 1989. preface.

13. William Carlos Williams. "The Use of Force." In William Carlos Williams. *The Doctor Stories.* New York: New Directions Books. 1984. (originally published 1932)

14. American Psychiatric Association. *Diagnostic and Statistical Manual of Mental Disorders.* 4th Edition. Washington, D.C.: American Psychiatric Association. 1994.


CHAPTER 2

1. Sidney Tarachow. *An Introduction to Psychotherapy.* New York: International Universities Press. 1963. pp. 153–187.

2. Brian Bird. *Talking With Patients.* New York: J.P. Lippincott and Company. 1973.

3. Frieda Fromm-Reichmann. *Principles of Intensive Psychotherapy.* Chicago: U. of Chicago Press. 1950.

4. Ralph Greenson. *The Technique and Practice of Psychoanalysis.* New York: International Universities Press. 1967.

5. Glenn Gabbard. *Psychodynamic Psychiatry in Clinical Practice.* 2nd Edition. Washington, D.C.: American Psychiatric Press. 1994.


CHAPTER 3

1. Leo Stone. *The Psychoanalytic Situation.* New York: International Universities Press. 1961.

2. Glenn Gabbard. *Psychodynamic Psychiatry in Clinical Practice.* Washington, D.C.: American Psychiatric Press. 1990. p. 10.

3. Willard Gaylin. *Caring.* New York: Knopf. 1976.

4. John Bowlby. *Attachment.* Vol. 1. 2nd Edition. New York: Basic Books. 1982.

5. Stanley Jackson. The listening healer and the history of psychologic healing. *Am. J. Psych.* 149:1623–1632.

6. Hayim Nahman Bialik. "Israel's Strength." In *Selected Poems.* New York: Bloch. 1948.

7. Jerry Kramer. *Instant Replay.* New York: New American Library. 1968.

8. Betty Rollin. *First You Cry.* New York: Signet. 1976.

9. Ethel Person. "Transference love." In *Dreams of Love and Fateful Encounters: The Power of Romantic Passion.* New York: Norton. 1988. pp. 241–265.

10. Linda and Ezekiel Emanuel. Four models of the physician-patient relationship. *JAMA.* 267:2221–2226. 1992.

11. Lewis Thomas. *The Youngest Science: Notes of a Medicine Watcher.* New York: Viking Press. 1983. pp. 12–26.

12. Richard Glass. The patient-physician relationship. *JAMA.* 275:147. 1996.

13. Robert Crenshaw and his colleagues. Patient-physician covenant. *JAMA.* 273:1553. 1995.

CHAPTER 4

1. Jerome Kagan and Herbert Moss. *From Birth to Maturity.* New York: Wiley and Sons. 1967. and George Vaillant. *Adaptation to Life.* New York: Little Brown and Company. 1977.

2. Burness Moore and Bernard Fine. *A Glossary of Psychoanalytic Terms and Concepts.* New York: American Psychoanalytic Association Committee on Indexing. 1968.

3. Richard Druss. Group intake conferences at a mental hygiene consultation service. *Military med.* 129:777. 1964.

4. American Psychiatric Association. *Diagnostic and Statistical Manual of Mental Disorders.* 4th Edition. Washington, D.C.: American Psychiatric Association. 1994.

5. Judith Rapoport. *The Boy Who Couldn't Stop Washing: The Experience and Treatment of Obsessive-Compulsive Disorder.* New York: E.P. Dutton. 1989.

6. John Oldham and Lois Morris. *New Personality Self-Portrait.* New York: Bantam Books. 1995.

7. American Psychiatric Association. *Diagnostic and Statistical Manual of Mental Disorders.* 4th Edition.

8. Gabriel Garcia Márquez. *Of Love and Other Demons.* New York: Alfred A. Knopf. 1995.

9. Lis Harris. *Holy Days: The World of a Hasidic Family.* New York: Summit Books. 1985.

10. Rapoport. *The Boy Who Couldn't Stop Washing.*

11. Lynn Payer. Borderline cases: How medical practice reflects national culture. *The Sciences.* 30:38–42. July-August, 1990.

CHAPTER 5

1. Carol Nadelson. "Issues in the analysis of single women in their thirties and forties." In John Oldham and Robert Liebert eds. *The Middle Years: New Psychoanalytic Perspectives.* New Haven: Yale U. Press. 1989. pp. 105–122.

2. Dinora Pines. The relevance of early psychic development to pregnancy and abortion. *Int. J. Psychoan.* 63:311–320. 1982.

3. Daniel Stern. *The Motherhood Constellation: Unified View of Parent-Infant Psychotherapy.* New York: Basic Books. 1995. pp. 171–190.

4. American Psychiatric Association. *Diagnostic and Statistical Manual of Mental Disorders.* 4th Edition. Washington, D.C.: American Psychiatric Association. 1994.

5. Katherine Phillips and her colleagues. Body dysmorphic disorders: 30 cases of imagined ugliness. *Amer. J. Psych.* 150:302–308. 1993.

6. Roger MacKinnon and Robert Michels. *The Psychiatric Interview in Clinical Practice.* Philadelphia: W.B. Saunders. 1971.

7. Sigmund Freud. *The Ego and the Id* (1923) in The Standard Edition of the Complete Psychological Works of Sigmund Freud. Vol. 19. Translated and Edited by James Strachey. London: Hogarth Press. 1962. pp. 3–63.

8. Wilhelm Hoffer. "Development of the Body Ego." *Psychoanalytic Study of the Child*. Vol. 5. New York: International Universities Press. 1950. pp. 18–33.

9. Paul Schilder. *The Image and Appearance of the Human Body*. New York: International Universities Press, 1950.

10. Lawrence Kolb. *Disturbances of the Body Image*. In American Handbook of Psychiatry. Silvano Arieti, editor-in-chief. New York: Basic Books. 1959.

11. Richard Druss and his colleagues. Psychologic response to colectomy. *Arch. Gen. Psych*. 18:513–519. 1968. and Richard Druss and his colleagues. Changes in body image following ileostomy. *Psychoan. Q.* 41:195–206. 1972.

12. Richard Druss and his colleagues. Psychologic response to colectomy II: Adjustment to a permanent colostomy. *Arch. Gen. Psych*. 20:419–427, 1969.

13. Richard Druss. Changes in body image following augmentation breast surgery. *Int. J. Psychoan*. 2:248–256. 1973.

14. Richard Druss. Cryptorchism and body image: The psychoanalysis of a case. *J. Am. Psychoan. Assoc.* 26:69–85, 1978.

CHAPTER 6

1. Sigmund Freud. *Lines of Advance in Psychoanalytic Therapy*. in the Standard Edition of the Complete Psychological Works of Sigmund Greud, Vol. 17. Translated and edited by James Strachey. London: Hogarth Press. 1962. pp. 165–166.

2. Jacob Arlow. The supervisory situation. *J. Amer. Psychoan. Assoc.* 11:576–594. 1963.

3. Helen Gediman and Fred Wolkenfeld. The parallelism phenomenon in psychoanalysis and supervision: its reconsideration as a triadic system. *Psychoan. Q.* 49:234–255. 1980.

4. Sara Cone Bryant. *Epaminondas and His Auntie*. New York: Buccaneer Books. 1976.

5. Daniel Levinson. *The Seasons of a Man's Life*. New York: Alfred A. Knopf. 1978.

6. Sigmund Freud. *Introductory Lectures on Psychoanalysis*. S.E. 16. 1917. p. 435,

7. Sigmund Freud. *New Introductory Lectures in Psychoanalysis.* S.E. 22. 1933. p. 80,


CHAPTER 7

1. Maria Sullivan. A synoptic historical review of the interface between psychiatry and religion. Psychiatry Grand Rounds, NYS Psychiatric Institute. New York, NY. June 4, 1997. unpublished.

2. David Lukoff and his colleagues. Toward a more culturally sensitive DSM-IV. *J. Nervous and Mental Diseases.* 180:673–682. 1992.

3. Sigmund Freud. *Obsessive Acts and Religious Practices* (1907) in the Standard Edition of the Complete Psychological Works of Sigmund Freud. Vol. 9. Translated and edited by James Strachey. London: Hogarth Press. 1962. pp. 117–127.

4. Sigmund Freud. *Totem and Taboo.* S.E. 13. 1913. pp. 1–162.

5. Sigmund Freud. *The Future of an Illusion.* S.E. 21. 1927. pp. 5–56.

6. Harold Koenig and his colleagues. Religious coping and depression among elderly hospitalized medically ill men. *Am. J. Psych.* 149:12. 1992.

7. Bradley Courtenay and his colleagues. Religiosity and adaptation in the oldest old. *Int. J. Aging and Human Development.* 34:47. 1992.

8. Rita Charon and her associates. Literature and medicine: contribution to clinical practice. *Ann. Intern. Med.* 122:599–606. 1995.

9. Jeffrey Levin and his colleagues. Religion and spirituality in medicine: research and education. *JAMA* 270:792. 1997.

10. Joseph Cardinal Bernardin. *The Gift of Peace.* Chicago: Loyola Press. 1997.

11. Ibid. p. 61.

12. Ibid. p. 70.

13. Richard Druss. *The Psychology of Illness: In Sickness and In Health.* Washington, D.C.: American Psychiatic Press. 1995.

14. Group for the Advancement of Psychiatry. *Caring for People with Physical Impairment. The Journey Back.* (Report 135). Washington, D.C.: American Psychiatric Press. 1993.

15. Simon Novick. *Milton Steinberg: Portrait of a Rabbi.* New York: Ktav Press. 1978.

16. Milton Steinberg. *Anatomy of Faith.* (Introduction by Arthur A. Cohen). New York: Harcourt Brace & Co. 1960.

17. Milton Steinberg. *A Believing Jew.* New York: Harcourt Brace & Co. 1951.

18. Ibid. p.318.

19. C.S. Cleeland. Undertreatment of cancer pain in elderly patients. *JAMA.* 279:1914–1915. June 17, 1998. Editorial.

20. Bernard Lown. *The Lost Art of Healing.* Boston: Houghton Mifflin. 1996.

21. Walter Benjamin. Healing by the fundamentals. *New Engl. J. Med.* 311:595. 1984.

CHAPTER 8

1. Richard Druss. "Healthy Denial." In *The Psychology of Illness: In Sickness and In Health.* Washington, D.C.: American Psychiatric Press. 1995. pp. 69–80.

2. Paul Wender and Donald Klein. *Mind, Mood and Medicine: A Guide to the New Biopsychiatry.* New York: Farrar, Straus and Giraux. 1981. pp. 329–342.

3. Ernest Ticho. Termination of psychoanalysis: treatment goals, life goals. *Psychoan. Q.* 41:315–333. 1972.

# Index